52 GREAT

BRIDGE TIPS

52 GREAT
BRIDGE TIPS

David Bird

B.T. Batsford • London

First published 2004

© David Bird 2004

The right of David Bird to be identified as Author of this work has been asserted by him in accordance with the Copyright, Designs and Patents Act 1988.

ISBN 07134 8892 1

A CIP catalogue record for this book is available from the British Library.

Typeset in the U.K. by Ruth Edmondson
Printed in the U.K. by Creative Print & Design, Ebbw Vale,Wales

for the publishers

B T Batsford, The Chrysalis Building, Bramley Road, London W10 6SP

An imprint of **Chrysalis** Books Group plc

Distributed in the United States and Canada by Sterling Publishing Co., 387 Park Avenue South, New York, NY 10016, USA

Editor: Elena Jeronimidis

CONTENTS

CONTENTS continued

Tip
1

Seek to combine two chances

It is amazing how often players ignore, or rather fail to spot, an additional chance to make a contract. Once they have identified a reasonable line of play, they go straight ahead without pausing to look more deeply into a hand. Our present Tip recommends that you seek to combine two chances. Would you have seen a second chance on this deal?

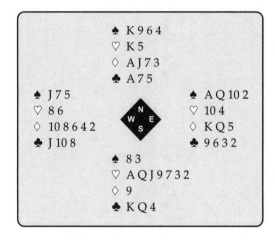

West leads a trump against your contract of 6♡. How will you play?

It seemed to the original declarer that everything would depend on finding West with the ♠A. He won the trump lead with the king and drew trumps in one more round. He then crossed his fingers and played a spade to the king. Finger-crossing proved an inadequate technique. East won with the ♠A and cashed a second spade trick to put the slam one down.

Declarer failed to spot a small extra chance in the diamond suit. If a defender happened to hold K-Q-x or K-Q doubleton, it would be possible to set up dummy's ◊J for a spade discard. To take advantage of such a lie of the cards, you need to preserve dummy's ♡K as an entry. You should win the trump lead in the South hand, cross to the ◊A and ruff a diamond low. You then cross to the ♡K and ruff another diamond.

When the cards lie as in the diagram, the extra chance materializes. The king and queen fall from the East hand, as if by magic, and dummy's ◊J is good. Because you made effective use of the ♡K as an entry, the ♣A still remains as an entry to dummy. After crossing to the club ace, you throw a spade loser on the ◊J and claim the contract. "I would have led a spade from your hand," East will tell his partner.

The possibility of ruffing down the king and queen of diamonds was an additional chance. If nothing came of it, as would usually happen, you could still lead towards the ♠K, taking your solid 50% chance there.

On the next deal you must discover whether your main chance will work, in order to play for the second chance.

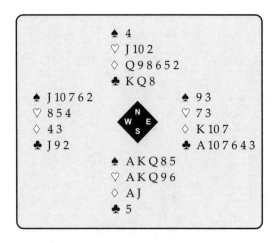

You win the trump lead against 6♡ and play a club to the king and ace. Back comes a trump. How will you continue?

If spades break 4-3, one ruff will suffice to establish the suit. Suppose you win the second trump, cash the ♠A and ruff a spade. Since you are hoping for a 4-3 spade break, you discard the ◊J on the ♣Q. You then return to your hand with the ◊A and draw the outstanding trump. Disappointment is in store. When you test the spades, they break 5-2 and you go one down. What went wrong?

There was only one entry to dummy – a spade ruff – and when you reached dummy you needed to know if the spades were breaking. So, the best play was to cash two rounds of spades before taking a spade ruff. When the 5-2 break came to light, you could then discard a spade on the ♣Q and take the diamond finesse for the contract.

Tip 2

Do not waste a high card in the third seat

If you spent an evening or two watching play at an average club, you would see many examples of incorrect play in the third seat. One of the most frequent errors would be that of wasting a high card. That's exactly what East did on this deal:

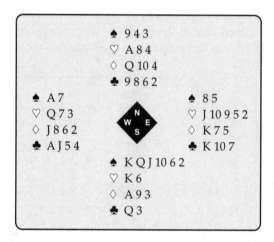

```
                 ♠ 9 4 3
                 ♡ A 8 4
                 ◊ Q 10 4
                 ♣ 9 8 6 2
   ♠ A 7                        ♠ 8 5
   ♡ Q 7 3          N           ♡ J 10 9 5 2
   ◊ J 8 6 2      W   E         ◊ K 7 5
   ♣ A J 5 4        S           ♣ K 10 7
                 ♠ K Q J 10 6 2
                 ♡ K 6
                 ◊ A 9 3
                 ♣ Q 3
```

Faced with a wretched choice of leads, West led ◊2 against South's spade game. Declarer played low from dummy and East played the king. At least half of the world's bridge players would make this mistake, you can be sure. The effect was not difficult to predict. Declarer won with the ◊A, knocked out the ace of trumps and eventually finessed the ◊10 for his contract. He lost just three tricks in the black suits.

Since you should not underlead an ace against a suit contract (see Tip 26), East can be certain that South holds the ◊A. It follows that there can be no purpose whatsoever in playing the ◊K at Trick 1. Declarer will clearly win three diamond tricks if East commits the king. He should play the ◊7 instead. South will win the trick with the ◊9, yes, but he will still have a diamond loser! The contract will go one down.

Here is a variation on that diamond suit – one where many defenders would go adrift:

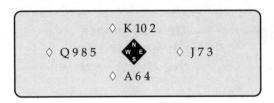

♢ K 10 2

♢ Q 9 8 5   ♢ J 7 3

♢ A 6 4

West leads the ♢5 and declarer plays low from dummy. If you waste the ♢J, you know that declarer will score three diamond tricks. Play the ♢7 instead and you will survive when partner's fourth-best lead was from ♢Q-9-8-5 and your ♢7 forces the ace. A slim chance is better than none!

Another common situation arises when dummy is short in the suit led and the release of a high card in the third seat will set up several winners in declarer's hand. Many defenders would go wrong on the East cards here:

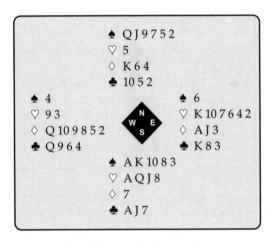

♠ Q J 9 7 5 2
♡ 5
♢ K 6 4
♣ 10 5 2

♠ 4   ♠ 6
♡ 9 3   ♡ K 10 7 6 4 2
♢ Q 10 9 8 5 2 ♢ A J 3
♣ Q 9 6 4   ♣ K 8 3

♠ A K 10 8 3
♡ A Q J 8
♢ 7
♣ A J 7

You pick up that promising East hand and are somewhat surprised when a 1♠ – 4♠ – 6♠ auction carries the opponents to a small slam. How will you defend when your partner leads the ♡9?

At your local club (you can bank on it) several East players would play the king at Trick 1. Third hand high, partner! The effect would be disastrous. Declarer would win with the ♡A and draw trumps. He would then throw two of dummy's club losers on the established queen and jack of hearts, making the slam.

When partner led the ♡9 it was clear that he did not hold an honour in the suit. East should have been able to see the ♡A-Q-J in South's hand. In that case it was obviously wrong to commit the ♡K at Trick 1, giving declarer three heart tricks. If East had played low instead, declarer would have made only two heart tricks. He would then have lost one diamond trick and one club, going one down in the slam.

When dummy has a sequence of honours in the suit led, you should think very carefully before covering in the third seat. Suppose your partner leads a diamond against a major-suit game and the diamonds lie like this:

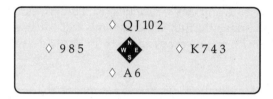

West leads the ◇8 (second best from a poor suit) and the ◇Q is played from dummy. It would be poor play to cover with the king. The purpose of covering an honour is to promote lower cards in your own hand or your partner's. Here you know that declarer holds the ◇A. If you cover you will give him three easy tricks. Play low and he will need two outside entries to dummy to achieve the same result (one to take a ruffing finesse with the J-10, another to reach the established card).

Let's change the suit slightly:

Partner leads the ◇6 and declarer plays low from dummy. Waste your ◇K and declarer will score four diamond tricks! Play low and he will need two outside entries to dummy to score three diamond tricks.

Tip
3

Draw two rounds of trumps to avoid an overruff

When dummy has three low trumps and you need to take a ruff there, you run the risk that one of the defenders will be able to overruff. You can reduce this risk by drawing two rounds of trumps before taking the ruff. Sometimes this will exhaust the holding of the defender who might otherwise overruff. That's the winning line on this deal:

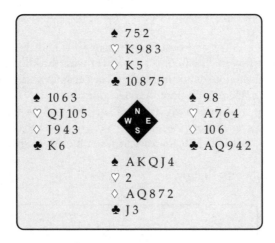

You arrive in 4♠ and West leads the ♡Q. It is inconceivable that West holds the ♡A, so you play low in the dummy. West persists with the ♡J and you ruff in the South hand. What now?

All will be well if the diamonds break 3-3. How can you give yourself a chance when the diamonds break 4-2? Suppose you cash the king and ace of diamonds and lead a low diamond on the third round, planning to ruff in dummy. That's no good, is it? The defender with a doubleton diamond will nearly always be able to ruff (or overruff) with a trump higher than dummy's ♠7.

You can improve your chances by drawing just two rounds of trumps with the ace and king. When both defenders follow, you cash the king and ace of diamonds and lead a low diamond from your hand. West

---

follows and you ruff in dummy. Luck is with you. East started with only two diamonds but he does not hold the last trump and cannot therefore overruff! You return to your hand by ruffing another heart, draw West's last trump and claim the contract.

What would have happened if trumps had broken 4-1 on that deal? Since you would not have been able to return to your hand with a second heart ruff (without losing trump control), you would have had to draw all the trumps and rely on a 3-3 diamond break.

When you do not hold all the top trumps, you may need to take special steps to allow you to draw precisely two rounds of trumps before attempting the critical ruff. Only a strong player would make the following contract.

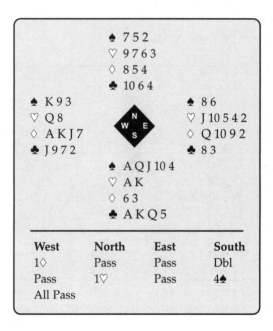

West	North	East	South
1◇	Pass	Pass	Dbl
Pass	1♡	Pass	4♠
All Pass			

West launches the defence with three rounds of diamonds. How will you play the contract?

You are almost certain to lose one spade trick, along with the two diamond tricks already lost. You must therefore avoid a club loser to make the game. All will be well if clubs break 3-3 or the ♣J falls in two rounds. How can you maximize your prospects when a defender holds ♣J-x-x-x? What you would like to do is to draw two rounds of trumps and then play the three top clubs. This would allow you to ruff the fourth club in dummy if the defender with the long clubs also started with three trumps.

What will happen if you play the ace and queen of trumps? West will win and may then play a third round of trumps, depriving you of your club ruff. The winning play is not easy to see. At Trick 4, you must lead the queen of trumps from your hand! West can win and play a second round of trumps but you still have one trump left in dummy. You play the ace and king of clubs, no jack appearing, and continue with the queen of clubs. If the suit happens to break 3-3, you will draw trumps and claim the contract. As the cards lie, East has only two clubs but – as on the previous deal – he does not hold the last trump and cannot therefore overruff. You ruff the ♣5 with dummy's last trump and return to your hand with a heart. Finally you draw West's last trump and claim the contract.

You would make the same sort of play here:

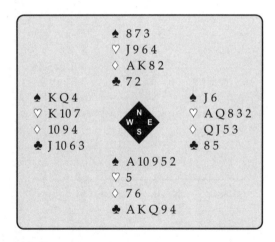

```
              ♠ 8 7 3
              ♡ J 9 6 4
              ◊ A K 8 2
              ♣ 7 2
♠ K Q 4                        ♠ J 6
♡ K 10 7          N           ♡ A Q 8 3 2
◊ 10 9 4      W       E       ◊ Q J 5 3
♣ J 10 6 3        S           ♣ 8 5
              ♠ A 10 9 5 2
              ♡ 5
              ◊ 7 6
              ♣ A K Q 9 4
```

West leads the ◊10 against your spade game. How will you play?

Suppose you win with the ◊A, cash two top clubs and ruff a club with the ♣8. That's no good. East will overruff from his doubleton trump and you will have three further losers. As on the previous deal, you need to draw precisely two rounds of trumps before taking the club ruff. Win the diamond lead and duck a round of trumps. When you regain the lead, draw a second round of trumps with the ace, cash two top clubs and ruff a club. Since the only outstanding trump is a master you don't mind at all if you are overruffed at this stage. You will make the contract easily, losing just two trumps and one heart.

Tip 4

Open light when you have a good suit

Nowadays players are willing to open on nearly every 12-count and will often make the first move on an 11-count. How should you judge whether a particular 11-count is worth opening? A valuable guideline is that you should open light when you hold a good suit.

Suppose you are first to speak, with neither side vulnerable. Which of these borderline hands is worth an opening bid?

(1)	(2)	(3)
♠ J 10 7 2	♠ J 2	♠ J 8 7 6 2
♡ 9 2	♡ A K 10 7 6 2	♡ A Q 2
◊ K Q J 9 2	◊ Q 10 2	◊ 8 5 2
♣ A 4	♣ 9 5	♣ K Q

Hand (1) contains only 11 points but a fine diamond suit. If you pass, the playing strength will not be present to overcall 2◊ on the next round. So, borrow a point and open 1◊ to make sure partner hears about the suit.

Hand (2) contains only 10 points, including a doubleton jack of dubious worth. Still, you have two potentially useful tens and a fine heart suit. Your hand is too strong for a weak two, even if you play this method, and you should open 1♡.

Hand (3) has a full 12-count, but just look at the number of negative features it contains. The club honours, crammed into a doubleton, are not worth 5 points. Nor are the heart honours particularly well disposed, being in a tripleton. There are no tens or nines at all and, worst of all, you would have to open 1♠ and would then be naming an extremely weak suit. You would be well advised to pass such a hand.

Let's move now to the third seat. When the first two players pass, what should your reaction be? The odds favour making some sort of opening bid now. If you pass, the opponents will have an easy time in describing their hands. However good their defensive bidding is, it is always easier to conduct an accurate auction when there is no competition. So, you

---

should open the bidding in the third seat whenever you reasonably can. It is less dangerous to open light than in the first two seats. Since partner is a passed hand, he is less likely to carry you too high.

Although you may be tempted to open many hands with only 9, 10 or 11 points, once again you should pay attention to the quality of the suit that you will be opening. The chances are high that you will be outbid eventually and when partner is on lead he may well decide to lead the suit that you have opened. It will be a nervous moment for you if your suit is something like Q-8-6-5-2 or K-9-6-2.

Which of these hands would you open in the third seat, at Love All?

(1)	(2)	(3)
♠ A K 10 7 2	♠ 8 2	♠ Q 8 7 6 2
♡ 8	♡ A 9 7 5 2	♡ A K J 10 5
◊ Q 9 8 3	◊ 10 5 2	◊ 3
♣ 10 5 3	♣ A Q 9	♣ 10 2

Hand (1) is what players call a 'good' 9-count. The honours are in the long suits and the singleton heart is a plus feature, giving the hand more playing strength than a 5-2-4-2 shape. You would not open the hand in the first two positions but in the third seat you should open 1♠.

Hand (2) is not worth an opening bid. The heart suit is relatively poor and your three honours will pull as much weight in defence as in attack. This brings to light another reason not to open on a bad suit. Partner may then misjudge how high to contest the auction. When your values are mainly outside the long suit, you will fare better defending. Partner will not be in on the secret when you have opened on a poor suit. He may decide to sacrifice and you will then go down, playing the hand, when your defensive values were enough to beat the opponents' contract.

Hand (3) is a problem. You have the values for a third-seat opening and with 5-5 shape you would normally open the higher of the two suits. The spades are weak, though. If you opened 1♠ and LHO eventually played in some contract, you would be worried that you had pushed partner towards a spade lead. Desperate to mention the hearts, some players would risk opening 1♡ or a weak 2♡, but neither of these is attractive. It is better to pass and hope that you can show your two-suiter later, perhaps with a Michaels Cue-bid.

Tip
5

Do not take
a hopeless finesse

Many a contract is squandered when the declarer takes a finesse that is absolutely certain to fail. Sometimes the bidding indicates this, sometimes the opening lead gives away the lie of the suit. On the first deal both of these indications were present.

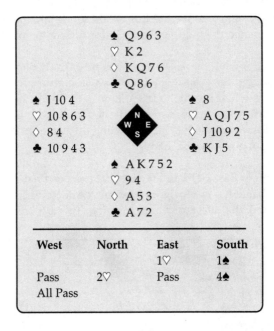

	North		South
West	North	East	South
		1♡	1♠
Pass	2♡	Pass	4♠
All Pass			

North's 2♡ cue-bid showed a sound raise to at least 2♠. South held a great hand for his one-level overcall, so he leapt to game on the second round. How would you play the spade game when West leads the ♡3?

Which card should you play from dummy? Ask yourself: can the king possibly win? There are two compelling reasons why the answer is 'No'. The first comes from the bidding. East opened the bidding and there are only 13 points missing, so he will surely hold the ♡A. The second clue comes from the fact that West has led the ♡3. No sensible player will underlead an ace against a suit contract. So, even if there had been no adverse bidding, you would be able to place the ♡A with East.

You should play low from dummy. East wins with the jack of hearts and cashes the heart ace. You win the jack of diamonds return and draw trumps in three rounds. Then you test the diamonds by cashing two more rounds of the suit. A 3-3 break does not materialise but all is well when it is East who hold the long diamonds. You lead dummy's last diamond and discard a club from your hand. East wins the trick and must now lead a club from the king or play a heart, which will give you a ruff-and-discard. Either way, you will make the contract.

Why do you choose this line of play, which depends on East holding the ♣K, instead of leading towards the ♣Q and playing West for the club king? Again the clue is in the bidding. With only 13 points missing and East having opened the bidding, he is almost certain to hold the ♣K.

You may wonder what can go wrong if you mistakenly play the ♡K from dummy at Trick 1. East can win with the ace and return to his partner's hand with a low heart to the ten. (He knows that West holds this card because his low spot-card lead (♡3) indicated an honour in the suit. See Tip 6.) West can now switch to a club, setting up a club trick for East and the contract can no longer be made.

Suppose dummy has A-Q-x in the suit that has been led and you have x-x-x in your hand. It is rarely right to commit the queen at Trick 1, whether or not you think that West may hold the king. This is a typical layout:

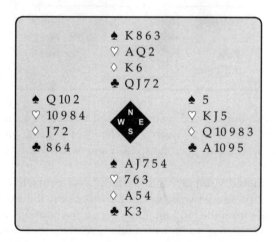

How would you play 4♠ when West leads the ♡10?

It's unlikely that West has led a heart from K-10-9-x. Even if he has, there is nothing to be gained by risking an immediate finesse of dummy's ♡Q.

You can see what will happen here, if you do play the queen. East will win with the king and clear a second heart trick for the defenders. You will then go down, losing two heart tricks, one trump trick and the ♣A.

To avoid this fate you must rise with the ♡A at Trick 1. You then play the king and ace of trumps, discovering that there is a loser in that suit. It is time to set up the club suit. You lead the king of clubs, continuing with a club to the queen if East ducks the first club. East cannot play a heart constructively from his side of the table. Whichever minor he plays instead, you will be able to discard one of your heart losers on the ♣J.

Suppose that West had held the ♡K all along. It would cost you nothing to rise with the ♡A at Trick 1. The defenders would still score one heart, one trump and the ♣A. The gain from playing the ♡A at Trick 1 came when the ♡K was wrong but East (the safe hand) held the ♣A. In other words you gave yourself two chances instead of one.

When a low spot-card is led through dummy's A-Q-x, it is often right to play dummy's low card. Your right-hand opponent will win the trick but cannot then continue the suit. That's what happens here:

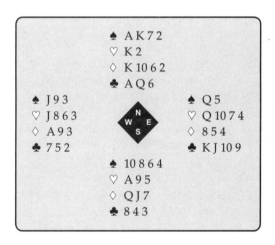

```
                    ♠ A K 7 2
                    ♡ K 2
                    ◇ K 10 6 2
                    ♣ A Q 6
    ♠ J 9 3                         ♠ Q 5
    ♡ J 8 6 3         N             ♡ Q 10 7 4
    ◇ A 9 3       W       E         ◇ 8 5 4
    ♣ 7 5 2           S             ♣ K J 10 9
                    ♠ 10 8 6 4
                    ♡ A 9 5
                    ◇ Q J 7
                    ♣ 8 4 3
```

West leads the ♣5 (second best from a poor suit) against your game in spades. How will you play the contract?

As on the previous deal, the dummy will eventually provide a discard. Your aim is to enjoy that discard before the defenders can score two club tricks. What will happen if you finesse the ♣Q at Trick 1? East will win with the king and clear the club suit. One down!

On the previous deal the answer was to rise with the ace of the suit that had been led. What will happen if you do that here? You draw two rounds of trumps, pleased to see a 3-2 break and then knock out the ace of diamonds. Luck is against you. It is West, the danger hand, who produces the diamond ace and a second round of clubs then spells defeat.

Only one play is good enough. You must play a low club from dummy at Trick 1. East wins with the ♣9 but he cannot safely continue the suit. When West plays another club, you rise with dummy's ace. Since West has to follow to two more rounds of diamonds, you will be able to discard your club loser on dummy's fourth diamond. Contract made!

Tip 6

Lead a high spot-card to show a weak suit

When you lead a new suit during the defence, it may be vital that your partner knows if you are leading from weakness or strength. To assist him, you should lead a high spot-card to show a weak suit.

The most important example of this is on the opening lead. A popular method of leading is known as 'second and fourth'. This means that you lead the fourth-best card when you are leading from a suit head by one or more honours (unless you have a sequence such as Q-J-10-x). For example, you lead the ♣4 from ♣K-J-7-4-2. From a suit headed by the nine at best, you lead the second-best card. So, you would lead the 7 from 9-7-3-2. The reason you don't follow the old 'top of nothing' method, leading the nine, is that your top card may be useful later in the play.

What is the purpose of letting partner know whether your suit is strong or weak? It's so that he knows whether he should return the suit when he gains the lead. Look at this typical deal:

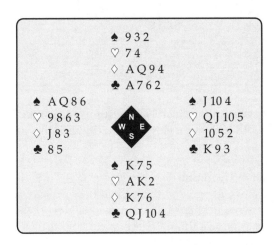

You are sitting East and your partner leads the ♡8 against 3NT. This is such a high spot-card that you are fairly sure he is leading from a weak suit. If you want to make sure, use the Rule of Eleven. Take 8 from 11 and this tells you that the two closed hands contain three cards higher than

---

the 8 (the ace, king and 9). It is barely possible that your partner has led from A-K-9-8(-x) and this chance is excluded when you play the ♡10 and declarer wins with the king. What should you do when declarer then runs the ♣Q to your ♣K?

Most defenders would press on blithely with the ♡Q. It is not good defence. It is very likely that declarer will then be able to run three club tricks, four diamonds and the two top hearts. Partner's ♡8 opening lead has told you that he has a weak suit there. You should therefore switch to spades, leading the ♠J. On this occasion you strike gold and defeat the contract. Whether or not your spade switch does happen to beat the game, it is the right thing to do! Some chance is better than none.

The same principle (a high spot-card lead shows a weak suit) can be used in the middle of the play. Here it is East who passes such a message.

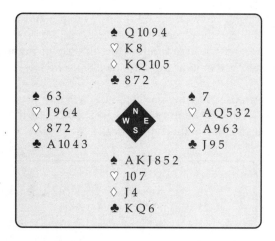

You are East again and partner leads a trump against 4♠. Declarer wins and leads the ◇J to your ace. How do you continue the defence?

If you can put partner on lead with a club, a heart switch is likely to defeat the game. The normal card to lead from J-x-x is the lowest card, because you are leading from three to an honour. If instead you were hoping that partner held ♣A-Q-10 and needed to score three club tricks, you would lead the jack through declarer, to hold the lead if he decided to duck. Here the right card is the nine of clubs.. This tells partner that you are weak in the club suit and would therefore like a switch to a different suit. When West wins with the ♣A, he should switch to a heart, defeating the contract. If instead you mistakenly led the ♣5, covered by the ♣Q and ♣A, West might well return a club, playing you for ♣K-J-5.

Tip
7

**Unblock a
high card to
create an entry**

I
t sometimes happens that you hold a very strong hand, as declarer, but the dummy is weak. In this situation you may need to take special steps to create the necessary entries to dummy. Would you have made 3NT here?

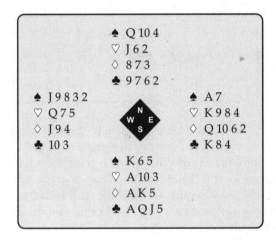

```
                    ♠ Q 10 4
                    ♡ J 6 2
                    ◇ 8 7 3
                    ♣ 9 7 6 2
    ♠ J 9 8 3 2              ♠ A 7
    ♡ Q 7 5          N       ♡ K 9 8 4
    ◇ J 9 4      W       E   ◇ Q 10 6 2
    ♣ 10 3           S       ♣ K 8 4
                    ♠ K 6 5
                    ♡ A 10 3
                    ◇ A K 5
                    ♣ A Q J 5
```

You reach a thin 3NT and West leads the ♠3. When you play low from dummy, East wins with the ♠A and returns a spade. How will you play?

I didn't like to give the answer away by asking you which card you would play on the first trick. The fact remains that unless you drop the ♠K under East's ace you will go down. To bring your total to nine you will need to score four club tricks. Unless East started with a doubleton ♣K, you will have to take two finesses against the king and will therefore need two entries to dummy.

Unblock the ♠K at Trick 1 and there is nothing the defenders can do. Suppose East switches to a diamond. You will win with the ◇A, finesse the ♠10 and finesse the ♣Q successfully. You will then return to dummy with the ♠Q and repeat the club finesse, making the game when the suit breaks 3-2. How could you be sure that a finesse against the ♠J would win? Nothing is certain in this life but West's lead of a low spot-card (the ♠3) strongly suggested that he was leading from an honour. Also, if East

---

held the ace and jack of spades he would have played the jack at Trick 1.

What will happen if you play a low spade from your hand on the first trick? You will then have only one entry to dummy (the ♠Q) and will not be able to finesse twice in clubs and pick up the suit. Does anything else occur to you about the deal? It would be a brilliant defence to find, but East can defeat you by refusing to take his ♠A at Trick 1! This would kill one of your entries to dummy.

A related technique is to win the first trick with a higher card than is necessary. Suppose West leads the ♡5 against 3NT here:

```
               ♡ Q J 4
♡ K 9 8 5 3    [N W E S]    ♡ 7 2
               ♡ A 10 6
```

You play low from the dummy, which is short of entries, and East contributes the ♡7. If you win the first trick with the ♡10, dummy's ♡Q-J will not provide an entry. It will be no good leading the ♡6 towards dummy because West will rise with the king, leaving your ace to win the third round. Instead you must win the first trick with the ace. Now you hold ♡10-6 opposite dummy's ♡Q-J and cannot be denied an entry to dummy in the suit.

Here is a full deal where such a technique – winning with a higher card than is necessary – creates a vital extra entry.

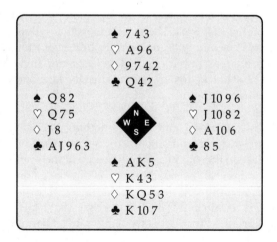

```
                    ♠ 7 4 3
                    ♡ A 9 6
                    ◇ 9 7 4 2
                    ♣ Q 4 2
♠ Q 8 2                           ♠ J 10 9 6
♡ Q 7 5          [N W E S]        ♡ J 10 8 2
◇ J 8                             ◇ A 10 6
♣ A J 9 6 3                       ♣ 8 5
                    ♠ A K 5
                    ♡ K 4 3
                    ◇ K Q 5 3
                    ♣ K 10 7
```

West leads the ♣6 against 3NT, East playing the ♣8. How will you tackle the contract?

With six tricks available outside diamonds, you will need to score three more tricks from from the diamond suit. East will have to hold the ◇A and if the card is twice guarded you will need to lead twice towards the honours in the South hand. To set up a second entry to dummy for this purpose, you should win the first trick with the ♣K rather than the ♣10. Do you see the difference this makes? With the king out of the way, you are certain to be able to cross the ♣Q later. If instead you retain the club king, West will rise with the ace when you subsequently lead the ♣7 from your hand and the king will have to take the third round. You will fare no better if you lead the ♣K on the second round, because West will hold up the ace.

So, after winning the first trick with the ♣K, you cross to dummy with the ♡A. A diamond to the king wins the next trick and you then lead a club towards dummy's queen. If West plays low, you will win with the ♣Q and lead another diamond towards your hand, setting up nine tricks. The only other option for West is to rise with the ♣A and clear the heart suit. As it happens, the hearts break 4-3, so the defenders cannot set up enough tricks to beat you. You win the heart switch, cross to the ♣Q and lead a diamond towards your hand. Again you make nine tricks.

Have you recorded this Tip deep in the brain somewhere? Remember that there are two ways in which you can set up an extra entry to dummy by playing a higher card than necessary from your own hand at Trick 1. When East wins the first trick, you can promote dummy's holding by dropping an honour from your hand. When instead East plays a lesser card you can sometimes benefit by winning the trick with a higher card than is necessary. Again the purpose is to promote the value of dummy's cards to ensure that you can cross to dummy in the suit later.

Tip 8

Raise responder's suit with three-card support

Suppose you open 1◇ and partner responds 1♠. Would you ever raise to 2♠ with only three-card support? This is one of the biggest differences between the bidding of good players and moderate players. In general, the better a player is, the more willing he is to raise on three-card support.

I can't prove to you that it's a good idea. You will just have to try it out and see for yourself how well it works. Let's look at a few hands to see how the method can pay off.

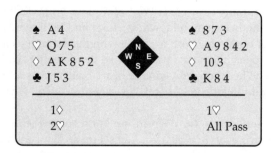

On part-score hands you can discover a 5-3 fit in a major. If instead you rebid 2◇ or 1NT on the West hand, there is no reason for East to insist on hearts and the fit will be lost.

Sometimes the knowledge of a fit may let responder head towards game:

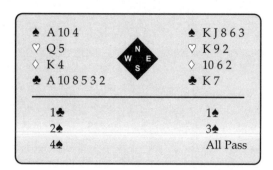

If West had rebid 2♣ instead, East would have let the bidding drop. When East hears of a spade fit, he sets his sights a little higher and invites game by bidding 3♠. West is happy to accept. He knows from the 3♠ game-try that East has five spades. With 11 points and only four spades, East would have bid 2NT instead.

What happens when responder is weak and has only four cards in his suit?

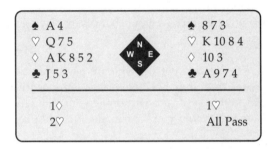

You end in a 4-3 fit. It's not the end of the world! There is a ruffing value in dummy. You have four tricks in the side suits and may well add four more in the trump suit. You might have done better in 1NT or 2◇, you might not. There is no need to fear a 4-3 fit, when playing at the two-level.

You don't want to play in a 4-3 fit at the four-level, it's true and when the responder is strong, he should not leap straight to the major suit game when he holds only a four-card suit. This is a typical auction:

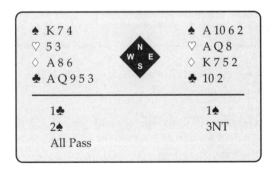

East has only four spades, so it would be a mistake to bid 4♠ on the second round. Since he has a stopper in both red suits, it is clear to rebid 3NT. West would usually correct to 4♠ if he held four spades. Since he has only three, he is happy to pass 3NT.

Tip 9

Play a false card at Trick 1

West makes his opening lead and East wins the trick. Is this the moment, as declarer, for you to switch off your concentration for a moment and follow with your lowest card? Usually, yes, but occasionally you can improve your chances by playing a false card at Trick 1.

The most common situation is when you are playing in no-trumps and are weak in a suit that your LHO (left-hand opponent) has failed to attack. Your aim in that case is to encourage your RHO to continue the suit that has been led. Would you have made the right play here?

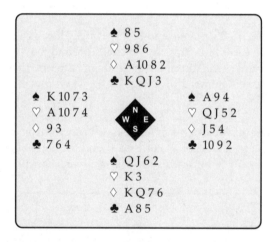

West leads the ♠3 against 3NT, East winning with the ace. What is your general plan to make nine tricks?

You can expect eight tricks in the minors and need to add one more from the majors. A spade return from East would suit you splendidly, since it would set up the extra trick that you need. It would also leave the safe (West) hand on lead. What would not suit you would be a heart switch from East. If West happened to hold the ♡A the defence would score at least four heart tricks and beat the contract before you had even gained the lead.

How can you encourage East to continue spades? Suppose you follow with the ♠2 at Trick 1. East will know then that his partner has only four spades (because the ♠3 is his fourth-best card and the ♠2 has already appeared). Since the defenders need five tricks to beat the contract, and these will probably have to come from the majors, East will surely conclude that he should switch to the ♡Q. Down you will go. Now see what happens if you follow with the ♠6 at Trick 1. East is likely to conclude that his partner has led from something like ♠K-J-7-3-2 or ♠K-10-7-3-2. In that case a spade return may be best.

Here is another example where you feign weakness in the suit led:

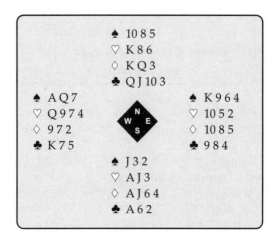

You open 1NT (15-17) and partner raises to 3NT. When West leads the ♡4, dummy plays low and East plays the ♡10. What is your plan?

Most players would win with the ♡J and cross to dummy with a diamond to run the ♣Q. When West won with the ♣K, he would (or should!) think on these lines: 'Declarer needs both red aces to bring his point-count up to 15. He therefore has three club tricks, three heart tricks and at least three diamond tricks. He is certain to make the contract unless partner has the ♠K and we can take four spade tricks.' He would then switch to the ♠A and the defenders would cash four spade tricks, beating the contract.

Suppose that you are more devious at Trick 1, winning East's ♡10 with the ace. Now West will place the ♡J with his partner. He will be able to count only eight certain tricks for you (two hearts, three diamonds and three clubs) and may well conclude that his best chance is to play another heart. The game will then be yours.

You can false-card in a suit contract too. The most common situation is when you fear that the opening lead is a singleton.

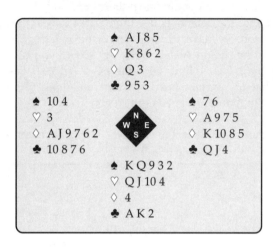

West leads the ♡3, a likely singleton, against your contract of 4♠. When East wins with the ♡A what is the best card to play from your hand?

If you follow with the ♡4, East can be fairly certain that the opening lead was a singleton. (The only other possibility would be from ♡Q-10-3.) How about playing the ♡Q, pretending that you have only one heart yourself? Is this a good idea? No, because if West held ♡J-10-4-3 he would have led the ♡J instead of the ♡3. The best card is the ♡J, making it look as if West has led from ♡Q-10-4-3. It is then at least possible that East will conclude that no further tricks are available from the heart suit. He may switch to the ♣Q, hoping that his partner has the ace and that the defenders can get rich in that suit.

Here is another situation to look out for:

East has overcalled in clubs and you are now playing in a major-suit game. West leads the ♣8, which is very likely to be a singleton. When East wins with the ♣J you should follow with the ♣10. If East believes that the opening lead was from ♣8-4, he may not continue the suit.

Tip 10

Signal your count when partner leads a king

What is your general method of signalling when partner leads a suit and you don't have to contribute your highest card in an attempt to win the trick? Do you give an attitude signal (where high encourages and low discourages)? Many players still use that type of signalling but an increasing number have switched to count signals (where high shows an even number of cards in the suit and low shows an odd number).

When partner leads an honour, you can get the best of both worlds by playing a system known as 'Ace for Attitude, King for Count'. In other words, when partner leads an ace (or queen) you give an attitude signal; when partner leads a king you give a count signal. It's a big topic and we will deal with it only briefly in this Tip. Let's start with a typical deal where a count signal can help you to defend correctly.

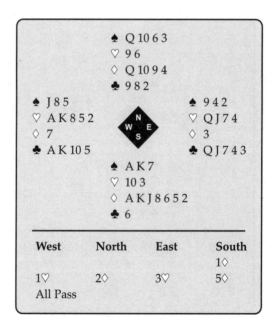

		♠ Q 10 6 3	
		♡ 9 6	
		◊ Q 10 9 4	
		♣ 9 8 2	

♠ J 8 5
♡ A K 8 5 2
◊ 7
♣ A K 10 5

♠ 9 4 2
♡ Q J 7 4
◊ 3
♣ Q J 7 4 3

♠ A K 7
♡ 10 3
◊ A K J 8 6 5 2
♣ 6

West	North	East	South
			1◊
1♡	2◊	3♡	5◊
All Pass			

Suppose you were sitting West, with your favourite partner across the table. Would you have defeated the contract?

Here is how the defence should go when you are playing 'Ace for Attitude, King for Count.' Since a heart lead is more likely to be ruffed, after partner's support of the suit, you lead a club. You may need to know how many clubs will stand up, so you lead the ♣K, asking for a count signal. Partner plays the ♣3, showing an odd number of clubs, and declarer follows with the ♣6. South is likely to hold a distributional hand for his leap to the five-level. He might hold three clubs (leaving your partner with three). It is perhaps more likely that he has only one club.

In any case, you don't have to take an immediate view in the suit. Partner would surely have bid more than 3♡ if he held six-card support for your hearts, so declarer is marked with at least one heart. At Trick 2 you play the ♡K, asking for a count signal in that suit. Partner plays the ♡7 and declarer follows with the ♡3. Since partner would not have played the ♡7 from Q-J-10-7-4, you know that declarer has another heart! You cash the ♡A and the game is one down. Had you tried to cash a second club instead, declarer would have ruffed, drawn trumps and thrown a heart loser on the fourth round of spades. Playing count signals saved you an unpleasant guess, one that you might well have got wrong.

Here is another full-deal example of gaining from a count signal:

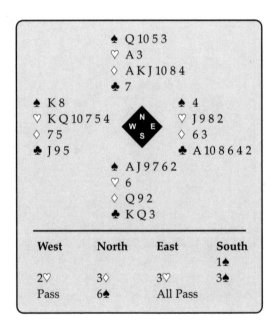

West	North	East	South
			1♠
2♡	3◊	3♡	3♠
Pass	6♠	All Pass	

North's bidding would not win any prizes, it's true, but how will you defend in the West seat? You lead the ♡K and dummy wins with the ♡A.

Declarer now runs the ♠Q and you win with the ♠K. What next?

Your answer should be: 'What count signal did partner give me at Trick 1?' Here he would play the ♡9, warning you that he holds four hearts. You will therefore switch to clubs, seeking the setting trick there. If instead partner played the ♡2, showing only three hearts, you would know that a second round of hearts would stand up.

When you lead a king against a notrump contract, the message is slightly different. You ask for a count signal, but **you also ask partner to unblock any honour that he holds** in the suit. The method would work well here:

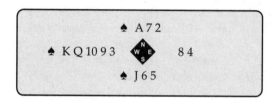

After an auction of 1NT – 3NT, you lead the ♠K against 3NT. The ♠2 is played from dummy, your partner playing the ♠8 and declarer the ♠5. What do you know about the lie of the suit?

The first point is that South must hold the ♠J. That's because your partner would have played the ♠J at Trick 1 if he held it (your king asked for 'unblock or count'). How many spades does East hold? His eight, a high card, is either the top of a doubleton, or a singleton. So, you know that South's ♠J is still guarded. Since a spade continuation will give declarer a second trick in the suit, you will switch to a different suit.

Now suppose this is the layout:

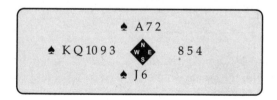

Again you lead the ♠K, declarer playing low in the dummy, but this time partner signals with the ♠4. It is now possible that he has three spades and that declarer started with a doubleton ♠J. You continue with the ♠Q, pinning South's ♠J and successfully clearing the suit. You are half-way towards defeating the contract!

Tip
11

Think before you finesse in trumps

I'm sure you know the standard guidelines on whether you should finesse in a suit when you are missing the queen. The recommended mantra is 'Eight Ever, Nine Never', meaning that you should generally finesse when you have a combined holding of eight cards but not when you have a combined holding of nine cards. When you are missing the king you should generally play for the drop with two cards out but finesse when there are three or more cards out.

When the suit involved is the trump suit, there are several reasons why you should not risk relinquishing the lead with a losing trump finesse. One such situation is when you are in danger of losing trump control. Would you have played the next deal correctly?

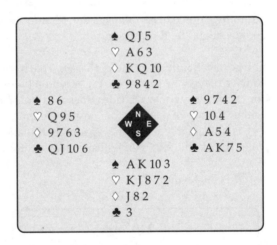

West leads the ♣Q against your game in hearts, winning the first trick. He persists with the suit and you ruff the second round. What next?

Suppose you think back to your bridge cradle and mutter to yourself: 'Eight Ever, Nine Never'. You cross to the ♡A and finesse the ♡J. The finesse will lose to West's queen. Are you worried now? You should be! When West plays another club you will have to ruff with your penultimate trump. When you draw the last trump and knock out the ♢A, East will cash a club trick. Nor will you fare any better if you knock out the ♢A first. East will then force your master trump with a club, promoting West's ♡9.

What went wrong? After taking one club ruff you had four trumps left and one of the defenders was bound to hold at least three trumps. You could not therefore afford the defenders to gain the lead twice more, once in trumps and once in diamonds, to force you again in clubs. The winning play, after ruffing the second round of clubs, was to cash the ace and king of trumps. So long as the trumps broke 3-2, you would then be safe. You could knock out the ♢A and still retain trump control. The defenders would be able to force you once more in clubs but not twice more.

Another situation when you should be wary of taking a trump finesse is when it will be into the dangerous hand. That's the case here.

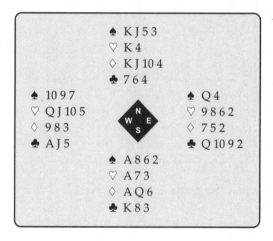

```
                    ♠ K J 5 3
                    ♡ K 4
                    ♢ K J 10 4
                    ♣ 7 6 4
    ♠ 10 9 7                       ♠ Q 4
    ♡ Q J 10 5          N          ♡ 9 8 6 2
    ♢ 9 8 3         W     E        ♢ 7 5 2
    ♣ A J 5            S           ♣ Q 10 9 2
                    ♠ A 8 6 2
                    ♡ A 7 3
                    ♢ A Q 6
                    ♣ K 8 3
```

West leads the ♡Q against your game in spades and you win with the ace. How will you continue?

Suppose you look at the spade suit in isolation and decide that a finesse is a good idea. You cash the ace of trumps and finesse the jack, losing to East's queen. East will switch to the queen or ten of clubs and you will lose three club tricks, going one down. Since East is the danger hand, the defender who can lead through your ♣K, you should take steps to keep him off lead. You should play the ace and king of trumps, spurning a finesse. Here the play will yield an unexpected bonus: the queen will fall doubleton from East. Suppose West had started with ♠Q-x-x, though. You would still make the contract. You would play four rounds of diamonds and discard one of your club losers. Even if East had started with ♠Q-x-x you would still have a good chance. If he had to follow to the first three diamonds, you could discard a club on the fourth diamond, not minding whether East ruffed with the master queen or not.

Another reason not to risk a trump finesse is because the defenders are threatening a ruff. Look at this deal:

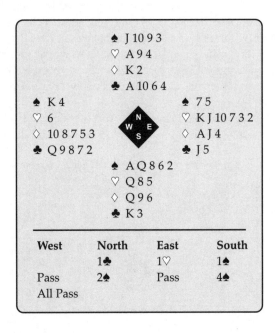

How will you play the spade game when West leads the ♡6?

It is too risky to play low from dummy. You can see what would happen when the cards lie as in the diagram. East would win with the ♡K and give his partner a ruff. West would then cross to the ◊A to receive a second ruff. You would not even receive a 'Bad luck, partner!' from across the table. East's overcall made it obvious that this could happen.

So, you rise with the ♡A at Trick 1. What next? If you finesse in the trump suit, you will suffer a similar fate. The finesse will lose to the king and West will lead a diamond to his partner's ace. East can then cash the ♡K and deliver a heart ruff for one down.

Playing in 4♠, you can afford to lose one trump trick but not two trump tricks. You should therefore play ace and another trump, rather than taking a finesse in the suit. West wins the second round of trumps with the king but cannot now score a ruff. When you regain the lead you will lead towards the ♡Q to make the contract.

Tip 12

Bid 1NT over a take-out double

What should you do when your RHO (right-hand opponent) makes a take-out double of your partner's one-bid and you have a balanced hand of 6-9 points? You don't have to bid, because partner will get another chance. Nevertheless, you should bid 1NT over the take-out double.

What is the point of this? By announcing at a convenient moment that you hold such a hand, you allow your partner to compete further over LHO's bid (if any). You also get the hand off your chest and avoid leaving yourself with a tricky problem on the second round of bidding. A third advantage is that you rob LHO of his chance to respond at the one level.

Suppose you are East and hold one of these hands:

(1)	(2)	(3)
♠ A 10 7	♠ K 8 2	♠ Q 8
♡ Q 8 6 3	♡ A J	♡ K J 5
◇ Q 9 8	◇ 9 8 6 3	◇ J 10 3
♣ 10 6 4	♣ J 10 7 5	♣ 10 8 7 5 2

West	North	East	South
1◇	Dbl	?	

On all three hands, you should respond 1NT. Some players would bid 1♡ on (1). It is the best bid if RHO passes, yes, but once he has doubled (suggesting four cards in each major) you should prefer a response of 1NT. On Hand (2) you have stoppers in each suit and 1NT is easily best. You are too strong for a jump to 3◇ and not quite strong enough for 2NT, which would show a limit raise in diamonds (10+ points). On hand (3) you are a bit concerned about the weakness in spades but you are still keen to describe your hand and prevent a cheap spade bid from South.

To appreciate the pre-emptive effect of these 1NT responses, let's see how the fourth player's action is made more difficult on these two South hands:

	(1)		**(2)**
♠	K Q 10 8	♠	A Q 8 6 2
♡	8 4	♡	10 3
◇	J 7 3	◇	9 7 2
♣	10 8 5 2	♣	K 7 4

West	North	East	South
1◇	Dbl	1NT	?

On (1) South would have greatly preferred a pass from you. He could then have told partner of the four-card spades, perhaps enabling further competition in that suit. As it is, he will either have to pass or to bid 2♠, which overstates his values. On (2) South has a different problem. If you had passed on the East cards, he could have expressed his hand well by jumping to 2♠. Now he is worried that 2♠ will not do full justice to his hand. That's because he would have to stretch (over 1NT) to bid 2♠ on hands a good bit weaker than this. In other words, he had been robbed of the chance to jump to 2♠ when 1♠ was available.

What can happen if you do not bid 1NT over the double? Suppose you elect to pass on the two East hands below and this situation arises:

	(1)		**(2)**
♠	Q 8	♠	K 7 3
♡	A 9 5	♡	J 10 4 3
◇	10 5 3	◇	9 7 2
♣	J 8 7 5 2	♣	K 7 5

West	North	East	South
1◇	Dbl	Pass	1♠
Pass	Pass	?	

You may think that no damage has been done, because you can re-open with a take-out double and partner will bid again. It's true in a way but because you allowed South to show his longest suit North may be able to compete to 2♠ and you have no reason to think that your side can play at the three-level. When the cards lie differently, North may raise to 2♠ before you have your second chance to bid. You will then be shut out on both these hands.

Tip 13

Look at the deal from dummy's viewpoint

Quite often you play in a major-suit game with a side suit such as ◊K-Q-x in the dummy and ◊A-x-x-x in your hand. If you have plenty of trumps in both hands, you can simply draw trumps and ruff the fourth diamond in dummy, if need be. Suppose you have five trumps in your hand and three in the dummy. You may then be able to draw just two rounds of trumps before playing on diamonds (See Tip 3). You can then ruff the fourth round of diamonds when the defender holding four diamonds also holds the last trump. This relies on luck, however, and there is sometimes a better way to play the hand. Look at this deal:

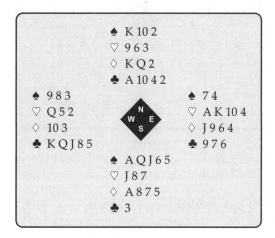

West leads the ♣K against your contract of 4♠. How will you play?

One possibility was discussed in the opening paragraph. After winning the club lead, you could draw two rounds of trumps and then play the three top diamonds. Here West would ruff the third diamond and you would go down.

Now look at the deal from dummy's point of view. What losers are there in the North hand? Three in hearts and three in clubs. If you can ruff all three clubs in the South hand, you will make the game! After winning

---

with the ♣A, you ruff a club immediately. You play the ace and ten of trumps, noting the 3-2 trump break, and ruff a second club. A diamond to the king permits a third club ruff and you return to dummy with the diamond queen to draw the last trump. Ten tricks are yours.

This play is known as a 'dummy reversal' because you treat your own hand as a dummy, taking ruffs there. On the deal we have just seen, you needed the trumps to break 3-2, otherwise you could not have drawn trumps with dummy's holding. Had trumps not broken 3-2, you would have reverted to the alternative line, playing on diamonds.

Let's see another example of this style of play:

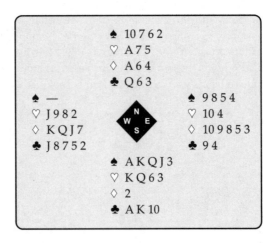

You reach the fine contract of 7♠. How will you play the grand slam when the ◇K is led to dummy's ace?

All will be well unless trumps are 4-0 because you will be able to draw trumps and ruff your fourth heart in dummy, if need be. What will happen if trumps are 4-0? If you look at affairs from the South hand, it may seem that you need the defender with the long trumps to hold at least three hearts. Now look at the situation from the dummy's point of view. The only losers are the two small diamonds! Ruff them in your hand and you will make the grand slam.

How does the play go? Because you are short of entries to dummy, you cannot make the grand slam unless you ruff a diamond at Trick 2! You then play the ace, king and queen of trumps, noting the 4-0 break. A club to the queen allows you to ruff dummy's last diamond and you return to the ♡A to draw East's last trump with the ten.

When declarer holds A-x-x in the suit that is led against no-trumps, he can often break the defenders' communications by holding up until the third round. Similarly, when the opening lead is won by the third player's ace and declarer holds K-x-x, he can hold up the king until the third round. Or can he? Defending in the third seat, you may have a chance to make life more difficult for declarer. By playing your middle card, instead of the ace, you may be able to knock out declarer's king and preserve communications with your partner.

Let's see an example of this style of play straight away. Take the East seat.

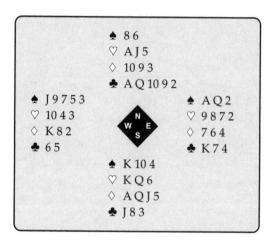

West leads the ♠5 against 3NT. Let's see what happens if you win with the ace. You return the ♠Q and declarer holds up the king, aiming to remove the spades in your hand. Declarer wins the third round of spades and now has a choice of finesses to take in the minors. Which one do you think he will choose? Yes, he will take the club finesse because it is 'into the safe hand'. The club finesse fails, as it happens, but the contract is still successful because you have no spade to return. When you switch to a diamond, declarer will rise with the ace and take his nine top tricks.

To beat the contract, you must aim to dislodge declarer's spade stopper on the first round. You can do this by playing the ♠Q on the first trick.

Declarer can hardly risk holding up the king now, because he might then lose the first five tricks if West's opening lead was from A-J-x-x-x. Once declarer has taken the ♠K, the defenders' communications are intact. Declarer can make the contract only by guessing which minor finesse is going to win. When the cards lie as in the diagram, no correct guess is possible and he will go down.

Note that the play of the ♠Q was correct only because you expected to gain the lead with the ♣K. When it is more likely that West would gain the lead, you would make the spade position clear to your partner by winning with the spade ace and clearing the suit. If instead you played the ♠Q at Trick 1, won by declarer's king, West might switch elsewhere when he gained the lead, concluding that declarer held the ♠A.

The same play is often right when you hold A-J-x in third position. Again your aim will be to drive out declarer's king, should he hold that card. Look at this deal:

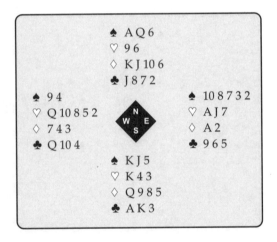

West leads the ♡5 against 3NT. How would you defend in the East seat?

There are three cards missing below partner's opening lead (the 4, 3 and 2 of hearts). It is therefore very likely that partner has a five-card suit. If you can force out declarer's heart stopper at Trick 1, you and your partner should be able to score four heart tricks when you gain the lead with the ◇A. You play the ♡J at Trick 1, therefore. As on the previous deal, declarer cannot afford to hold up the ♡K or he risks losing five immediate heart tricks. His best chance, so far as he can see, is to win the first heart trick and then to knock out the ◇A. He will then make the contract when the hearts split 4-4. As the cards lie, he will go down.

52 Great Bridge Tips

When you win with the ♦A you will play ace and another heart, allowing your partner to run the rest of the hearts.

Perhaps you are thinking that such a defence might give declarer an undeserved trick if he held the ♡Q instead of the ♡K. It's true but the contract would still go down (which is your primary concern as a defender), as long as your partner had four heart tricks to take when you won with the ♦A. It is most unlikely that declarer could score eight black-suit tricks and make the game without playing on diamonds.

We can draw one more instructive point from the deal. What if your partner had led the ♡2, instead of the ♡5? Knowing that he held only four cards in hearts, you could not afford to play the ♡J and perhaps concede a trick to declarer's ♡Q-x-x. You would win with the ♡A and return the ♡J, hoping that your side could score four heart tricks and the ♦A.

Tip 15   With an A-J-x stopper see which defender will gain the lead

Y ou are playing in 3NT and West leads a spade, where you hold x-x in the dummy and A-J-x in your hand. When East puts up one of the big honours, should you win the trick or duck? Your decision will normally depend on which defender is likely to gain the lead later in the play. If West will gain the lead, you should win the first trick, retaining your J-x as a second stopper against him. If instead East is likely to gain the lead, you should play low on the first trick, planning to hold up the ace until East's holding in the suit is exhausted.

Let's look at some full deals to see how you can calculate whether or not to win the first trick. What would your decision be here?

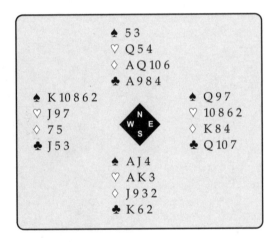

West leads the ♣6 against 3NT, East producing the ♠Q. How will you play?

You have seven tricks on top and will have to take the diamond finesse in order to set up the extra tricks that you need. Which defender might gain the lead when you do this? East! So, you should hold up the spade ace until the third round, aiming to exhaust East of his spade holding. When you then take the diamond finesse, it loses. Since you made the right play in spades this is no problem. East has no spade to play and you make the game easily. If East had held another spade the suit would have broken 4-4 and you would lose only one diamond and three spades.

Suppose we switch the North and South diamond holdings, so that it is West who may gain the lead. This might be the layout:

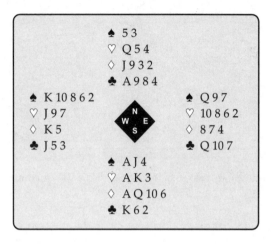

Again you are in 3NT and West leads the ♠6 to East's queen. How will you play this time?

You have the same seven tricks and will have to finesse in diamonds as before, but now it is West who may gain the lead. You must therefore play differently at Trick 1! You win East's ♠Q with the ace, retaining your ♠J-4 as a second stopper against West. You cross to dummy with a heart or a club and run the ◊J. Your claim to be the world's unluckiest player is given some credence when the diamond finesse loses. Since you made the right play at Trick 1, this does not matter. West is on lead and cannot play a spade without setting up your jack. On any other return you will be able to claim nine tricks and the contract.

Finally let's look at a deal where you have a choice of finesses to take for the extra trick that you need.

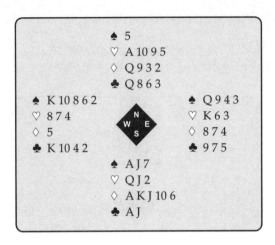

```
                    ♠ 5
                    ♡ A 10 9 5
                    ◇ Q 9 3 2
                    ♣ Q 8 6 3
  ♠ K 10 8 6 2           N           ♠ Q 9 4 3
  ♡ 8 7 4            W       E        ♡ K 6 3
  ◇ 5                    S            ◇ 8 7 4
  ♣ K 10 4 2                          ♣ 9 7 5
                    ♠ A J 7
                    ♡ Q J 2
                    ◇ A K J 10 6
                    ♣ A J
```

West leads the ♣6 against 3NT and East plays the queen. How will you play?

Once again you must make a plan for the whole contract before deciding how to play at Trick 1. Since you hold only four spades between the two hands, it is much less likely that you can exhaust East's spades by holding up for two rounds (spades would have to break 6-3 or 7-2). A better idea is to win the first round of spades with the ace and then attempt to keep East off lead.

You have eight top tricks and therefore need only one more for game. Once you have won the first spade trick with the ace, East is the danger hand. If you finesse in hearts and this loses, a spade return will defeat the contract. Instead you should cross to dummy with a diamond and finesse the ♣J. This finesse loses too, but it causes no problem. The safe (West) hand is on lead and cannot profitably play on spades. If he switches to a heart you will rise with dummy's ace and claim nine tricks.

Did you notice that six diamonds was cold on the hand above? All the more reason not to go down in 3NT!

Tip
16

Support immediately when you are weak

O ne of the most valuable actions you can take during the auction is to support your partner's suit. This is particularly true when you are weak and may not get the chance to make another bid. After a start of 1◊ – Pass, what would you respond on these two hands?

(1)	**(2)**
♠ 10 2	♠ 6 5
♡ K J 8 4	♡ J 8 7 3
◊ A Q 8 5	◊ A J 6 2
♣ A 7 2	♣ 10 7 3

On (1) you have 14 points and there will be plenty of time to investigate the best contract. There are several reasons why 1♡ is the best response. You may discover a 4-4 heart fit. The response in hearts may also allow your partner to bid notrumps. Apart from anything else, you cannot raise diamonds directly because 3◊ would be non-forcing and 4◊ (not that you would consider this) would carry you past 3NT.

Everything changes on (2). Most text books say 'always show a four-major at the one-level' but it is not the best move on such a weak hand. Why is that? With 6 points you are likely to get only one bid. You should use this to describe your hand accurately, raising to 2◊.

What can go wrong if you respond 1♡? Firstly, your partner may raise to 2♡ with three-card support (see Tip 8). You will have to pass and you may have missed a 5-4 diamond fit. More likely is that the opponents will enter the bidding and the auction will have reached 2♠ by the time it comes back to you. You can hardly bid 3◊ then because partner would expect more than 6 points. If instead you raise to 2◊ at your first turn, all will be well. Partner can compete further in diamonds when he has some shape or values to spare. (If you play a five-card major system and a 1◊ opening bid can be made on a 3-card suit, the scales tilt the other way. Since you cannot be sure of an 8-card diamond fit, respond 1♡.)

The same applies when you hold four spades and partner opens 1♡. The next player passes and you must find a response on one of these hands:

(1)	(2)
♠ A K 8 2	♠ K 8 7 2
♡ K 7 3	♡ Q 9 6
◇ 9 2	◇ J 10 8 2
♣ J 10 7 2	♣ 10 5

On (1) you are going to make a second bid. Respond 1♠ with the intention of giving jump preference to 3♡ over partner's rebid of 2♣ or 2◇. You would respond 1♠ if the hand was stronger, too. You would want to find out as much as possible about partner's hand and the easiest way to do this is by responding in a new suit and waiting for his rebid.

Many players would respond 1♠ to 1♡ on (2), as well. It is much better to raise to 2♡, even if you are playing a four-card major system. You are worth only one bid and partner will be grateful to know of heart support if the fourth player enters the auction. Suppose the bidding continues:

West	North	East	South
1♡	Pass	2♡	3♣
?			

Your partner is ideally placed. He can bid 4♡ with a strong hand, compete to 3♡ with extra shape, or perhaps suggest a game by bidding 3◇. Compare West's happy situation after a 2♡ response with this:

West	North	East	South
1♡	Pass	1♠	3♣
?			

Now the opener has no idea of your overall strength. On certain strongish hands he may be tempted to bid 3♠ on three-card support, hoping that you have five spades. Nor does he know of your heart support. He cannot therefore compete to 3♡ on a moderate hand with six hearts. Even if West and North both pass, you will be poorly placed. You want to support partner's hearts but you are nervous of doing so on 6 points because a three-level bid will suggest at least 9 points.

Tip 17

Lead towards honours to avoid a ruff

Sometimes a side suit breaks badly, with one of the defenders holding a singleton. By leading towards your honours in the suit you may be able to prevent them from being ruffed. This type of deal occurs frequently:

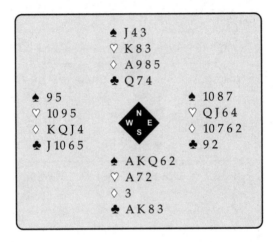

♠ J 4 3
♡ K 8 3
♢ A 9 8 5
♣ Q 7 4

♠ 9 5
♡ 10 9 5
♢ K Q J 4
♣ J 10 6 5

♠ 10 8 7
♡ Q J 6 4
♢ 10 7 6 2
♣ 9 2

♠ A K Q 6 2
♡ A 7 2
♢ 3
♣ A K 8 3

West leads the king of diamonds against 6♠. How will you play it?

You win the diamond lead with dummy's ace and play the ace and king of trumps, pleased to see the 3-2 trump break. If clubs break 3-3 all will be well. You can give yourself an extra chance by playing on clubs before you draw the last trump. You should play the clubs in a special way to avoid having one of your honours ruffed, should East hold a doubleton in the suit. You cash the club ace, cross to the queen and lead a third round towards your king.

East has no answer to this. If he ruffs in, your king of clubs will survive. You can use it to discard a heart from dummy and eventually ruff a heart for the twelfth trick. If instead East declines to ruff, you will win the third round of clubs with the king and ruff a club with dummy's ♠J. You can then return to your hand with the ♡A, draw the last trump and claim twelve tricks, losing one trick in hearts.

What was the most important move on that hand? Leading the third round of clubs towards your remaining honour. Had you led the king from hand instead, East would have ruffed and you would then have an inescapable further loser in hearts.

On the next deal an opening bid from West warns you of a bad break in the heart suit. How will you take advantage of this information?

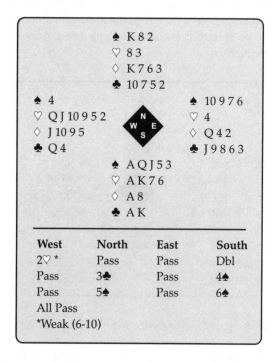

West	North	East	South
2♡ *	Pass	Pass	Dbl
Pass	3♣	Pass	4♠
Pass	5♣	Pass	6♠
All Pass			

*Weak (6-10)

West opens with a Weak Two bid and subsequently leads the ♡Q against your small slam in spades. How will you play the contract?

You win the opening lead with the ♡A and must somehow dispose of one of your heart losers. That won't be possible if you draw trumps straight away because you need to ruff at least one heart in the dummy. Suppose you play the ♡K at Trick 2. That's no good either, because East will ruff and still be in a position to overruff the dummy when you ruff one of your remaining heart losers with the ♠8.

Instead you must cross to dummy with the ♢K and lead a second round of hearts towards your hand. There is nothing East can do! If he ruffs a loser, your ♡K will live to fight another day and you can ruff your only remaining heart loser with dummy's ♠K. Let's suppose that East

52 Great Bridge Tips

discards instead and you win the second round of hearts with the king. You ruff a third round of hearts with the king, return to your hand with a club honour and ruff the last heart with the ♠8. Whether or not East overruffs at this stage, he will score just one trump trick and you will make the slam. By leading **towards** your second heart honour, you prevented East from ruffing it.

Do you see why it was important to ruff the last heart near the end, even though you knew you would be overruffed? It was because East's 10-9-7-6 in the trump suit had been promoted into a trick when you ruffed a heart with dummy's king. By forcing him to overruff, you avoided losing both a heart trick and a trump trick.

On the final deal you have to lead twice towards a key honour holding.

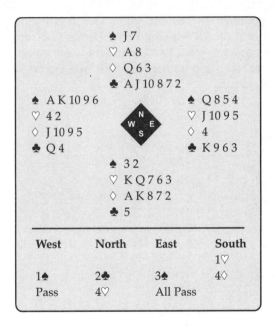

| ♠ J 7 |
| ♡ A 8 |
| ◇ Q 6 3 |
| ♣ A J 10 8 7 2 |

♠ A K 10 9 6   ♠ Q 8 5 4
♡ 4 2   ♡ J 10 9 5
◇ J 10 9 5   ◇ 4
♣ Q 4   ♣ K 9 6 3

♠ 3 2
♡ K Q 7 6 3
◇ A K 8 7 2
♣ 5

West	North	East	South
			1♡
1♠	2♣	3♠	4◇
Pass	4♡	All Pass	

You arrive in game on a 5-2 fit and West cashes his two top spades, switching to a trump. How will you play the hand?

If diamonds break 3-2 you can afford to lose a trick in the trump suit. If diamonds are 4-1 it may seem that you will need a 3-3 trump break. On this particular hand there is an extra chance. Seeing that you may need to ruff the fourth round of diamonds in dummy, you win the trump switch with dummy's ace. You then play the queen of diamonds and lead a second round of diamonds towards your hand. What can East do? If he ruffs, he will ruff a diamond loser rather than an honour. He will expend his natural trump trick and you will make the contract easily. Let's suppose he discards instead and your ◇A wins the trick. What now?

You return to dummy with the ace of clubs and lead another diamond towards your hand. Once again East cannot gain by ruffing a loser with his natural trump trick. He discards and you win with the ◇K. Now the great moment has come. You ruff your fourth round of diamonds with dummy's ♡8! If East overruffs, the defenders will take no further trick. If instead he discards, you will ruff a club to your hand and draw two more rounds of trumps. You can then lead the established card in diamonds to force out East's master trump. Ten tricks will be yours.

It was essential to lead towards the ace and king of diamonds, so that East had no chance to ruff an honour. Play the hand any other way and you would go down. By the way, do you see how the defenders could have beaten the contract? Suppose West switches to a trump at Trick 2. If you play the same way now, East can ruff the second diamond and cross to partner's ♠K for a second diamond ruff. You would have no way to make the contract.

Tip 18

When in doubt lead an unbid suit

Have you heard of the guideline: when in doubt, lead a trump? It's no good! There are a few situations in which a trump lead may work well (when a take-out double at the one-level has been passed out, when responder has given preference to declarer's second suit, when you have a great balance of the points and the opponents are sacrificing). 'Being in doubt' is not one of those situations! A much more sensible general guideline is to attack in an unbid side suit.

What's more, you cannot wait until you have a pristine Q-J-10-x in an unbid suit. You must be willing to lead from holdings such as K-J-x-x or K-10-x-x. If any player tells you that he doesn't like leading from a king, nod politely but mark him down as someone who will never achieve much at the game. Deals such as the following arise by the thousand:

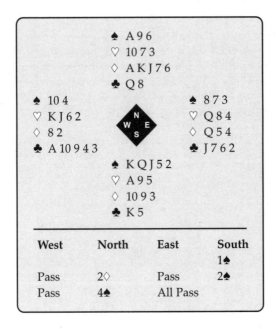

West	North	East	South
			1♠
Pass	2◊	Pass	2♠
Pass	4♠	All Pass	

You are on lead against South's spade game. How do you think declarer will play the contract? You cannot be sure but it sounds from the bidding as if declarer will set up dummy's diamonds and then take some discards. You must hurry to set up your own tricks before he can do this.

Let's see first what will happen if you are a 'when in doubt lead a trump' follower. Declarer will win the trump lead, draw trumps and run the ♢10. The finesse will lose but declarer is assured of eleven tricks. His two heart losers will be thrown on the long cards in dummy's diamond suit.

All of this was entirely predictable! West should have made an attacking lead in one of the unbid suits, hearts or clubs. Since it is rarely right to lead an ace, except when you hold an A-K combination (see Tip 26), it is clear to lead the ♡2. You can see how well it works here. Declarer cannot avoid the loss of two hearts, one diamond and one club.

Are you still a bit dubious about this? Are you saying to yourself: 'What if declarer held the ace-queen?' It's quite possible that declarer will hold the ace and queen of hearts between the hands, but in that case you probably couldn't beat the contract anyway. When dummy has announced a long side suit, the best lead in the long run is to attack in one of the unbid suits. If the previous deal arose in some top championship, you can be sure that nearly every West would lead a heart. It's as clear-cut as that.

If you're still not sure, think of it this way. If you held K-Q-J-x in an unbid side suit, you would think it one of the best leads in the world. So it is. But when you hold K-J-x-x and partner has the queen, the lead is just as effective! If you lead an 'in doubt' trump, most contracts will be made anyway. So, there is not much to lose by making an attacking lead in a side suit. Let's see one more example:

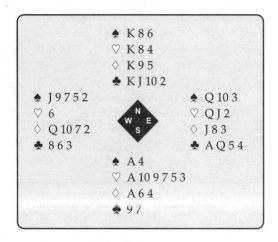

West	North	East	South
			1♡
Pass	2♣	Pass	2♡
Pass	4♡	All Pass	

You are sitting West, not overjoyed at having picked up a mere 3-count. What should you lead against 4♡?

You need to attack in one of the side suits. Is it better to lead a spade or a diamond. There are two reasons why a diamond is better. Can you think of them? The first is that you hold five spades and only four diamonds. It is therefore slightly more likely that one of the opponents will be short in spades and you will not be able to score many tricks in that suit. The second reason is that your own diamonds are stronger than the spades. You will therefore need less help from partner to set up a trick or two.

You lead the ◇2, then, and partner dutifully produces the ◇J. Declarer is a doomed man. He wins with the ace and draws two rounds of trumps with the king and ace, discovering that he has a loser in that suit. When he runs the ♣9, partner wins with the ♣Q and returns a second round of diamonds, knocking out dummy's king. Declarer has no option but to play another club, but East wins with the ace and plays a third round of diamonds. Yes! It was hard work but your diamond lead paid off eventually. You have scored one trump, two clubs and a diamond, beating the contract by one trick.

There were sound logical reasons for choosing a diamond lead on that deal. Of course, such a lead would not always be successful. Occasionally a spade lead would have worked better, or even some other lead. (You would then be cursing the day that you decided to buy some Batsford book of Bridge Tips.) In the long run, though, a diamond lead would fare best.

When you are playing in a suit contract and are worried about losing too many tricks in one of the side suits, you can sometimes force the defenders to play the suit for you. When they make the first play in a suit, your prospects there will never be worse and will usually be much better.

For example, suppose you hold ◊Q-6-4 in the dummy and ◊J-8-2 in your hand. If you have to play the suit yourself, you are likely to lose three diamond tricks whenever the ace and king lie in different hands. If you can force the defenders to play the suit, you are certain to score a trick. How can you achieve this aim? By eliminating one or more side suits and then throwing a defender on lead. Let's see how this is done. Almost half the field went down when the deal below arose in a local duplicate:

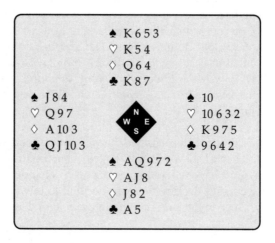

West leads the ♣Q against 4♠. How would you plan the play?

Suppose you win the club lead, draw trumps and take the heart finesse. It loses and West exits safely in hearts. You will have to tackle the diamonds yourself and, with the honours split, you will lose three further tricks. That's one down.

You would like to force the opponents to make the first play in diamonds. How can this be done? After winning the club lead and drawing trumps, you must eliminate the club suit. What does that mean? You cross to the ♣K and ruff a club in your hand. Since this leaves you with no clubs in either hand, the defenders will not be able to play that suit. (If they did, it would give you a ruff-and-discard.) What do you do next? Take the heart finesse? No, because if it loses, West will probably have a safe heart return. Instead you must cash the king and ace of hearts and exit with the ♡J. It makes no difference which defender wins the third round of hearts. He will have to play a diamond (or give you a ruff-and-discard).

When you have a holding such as A-Q-2 in your hand, you would like the player on your left to lead the suit. (It would not help you if your RHO made the first play in the suit, through the tenace.) Sometimes you can throw a specific defender on lead with the last card in a different suit. That's what happens here:

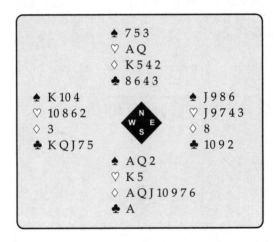

You bid to 6◇ in splendid fashion (in truth, it was a fairly rustic sequence: 1◇ – 3◇ – 6◇) and West leads the ♣K. How will you plan the play?

There are two possible losers in spades and you would like to force West to lead this suit. You can achieve this when West has five or more clubs. You win the club lead, draw trumps with the ace and cross to the ♡Q to ruff a club. You then play the ♡K to the ♡A and ruff another club. Finally you reach dummy again with the king of trumps and survey this end position:

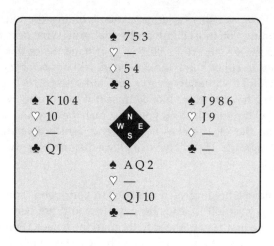

You lead dummy's last club and East discards. Success is now guaranteed. Instead of ruffing the club, you discard a spade loser. West wins the trick and has no safe return. He must either lead a spade into your ace-queen or play his last heart, giving you a ruff-and-discard.

Sometimes you can even perform the throw-in in the trump suit:

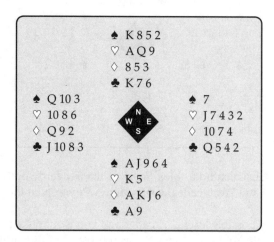

West leads the ♣J against your small slam in spades. Instead of taking an immediate view in trumps, cash the ♠K and eliminate both clubs and hearts. You then plan to finesse the ♠J. If West wins with a doubleton ♠Q, he will have to play a diamond (or give you a ruff-and-discard). When East shows out on the second trump, you win with the ace and throw West on lead with the third round of trumps. Again he must play a diamond into your tenace or give you a ruff-and-discard. Twelve tricks!

Tip 20

Don't double when the opponents may run

The opponents bid to some game or slam and you can tell from the cards in your own hand that they are fairly certain to go down. Should you make a penalty double? The first point to note is that a double does not bring a very high reward when the contract goes only one down. Scoring 100 instead of 50, or 200 instead of 100, is not much of a difference. If they were in a silly contract, you were booked for a great board anyway! There are two situations where a double can prove incredibly expensive. One is where they make the doubled contract only because of the information given away by your double. The other is where they decide to run to some different contract, which proves unbeatable. Both situations can give you nightmares (take my word for it!) Let's see some examples of unwise doubles.

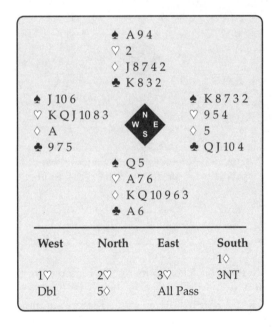

	♠ A 9 4	
	♡ 2	
	◇ J 8 7 4 2	
	♣ K 8 3 2	

♠ J 10 6   ♠ K 8 7 3 2
♡ K Q J 10 8 3   ♡ 9 5 4
◇ A   ◇ 5
♣ 9 7 5   ♣ Q J 10 4

	♠ Q 5	
	♡ A 7 6	
	◇ K Q 10 9 6 3	
	♣ A 6	

West	North	East	South
			1◇
1♡	2♡	3♡	3NT
Dbl	5◇	All Pass	

North's 2♡ showed a sound limit raise in diamonds (see Tip 24). West could not believe his luck when South bid 3NT. Surely this would go down on a heart lead. It was very unlikely that declarer would be able to score eight tricks in the black suits, to go with the heart ace. This analysis of South's prospects in no-trumps was faultless. What was not faultless was West's conclusion that he ought to double 3NT. North might well have been intending to pass 3NT. Once he heard the double, he took flight into the diamond game. So, West ended with a score of minus 600 instead of the plus 200 that he would probably have scored, had he had the presence of mind to pass 3NT.

Terence Reese used to quip that when you pass a contract that you are sure will fail, you should do so with the 'air of a man going to his own funeral'. In other words, you should give nothing away. If you think for a while about doubling, the damage is done. Even if you eventually pass, the opponents may conclude that you have the beating of the contract in your own hand and that they may do better elsewhere.

The second example of an unwise double arose in a pairs championship.

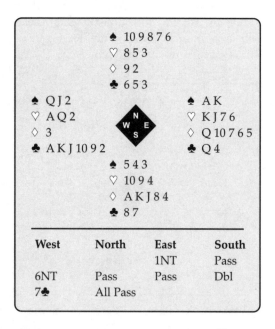

West	North	East	South
		1NT	Pass
6NT	Pass	Pass	Dbl
7♣	All Pass		

South found himself on lead against 6NT, holding the ◊A-K. Having checked that it was not just a pleasant dream, he doubled. West headed for cover in 7♣ and South's dream turned into a nightmare as partner agonised over what to lead. A heart was the choice and 7♣ was made.

(Did you say to yourself "What a ridiculous 6NT bid! No-one would bid so poorly at our club"? East-West were the Poles, Piotr Gawrys and Krzysztof Jassem, one of the world's strongest pairs!)

Tip
21

Cash the top cards to maximise your chance in a suit

The best way to play a particular holding in a suit often varies according to how many tricks you need from it. If you need the maximum — four tricks out of four, for example — you may have to hope for one particular distribution of the cards. If three tricks from the suit will suffice for the contract, you must look for a safety play that maximises the chance of achieving those three tricks. Often such safety plays involve cashing the high cards in a suit rather than taking an early finesse.

Let's start with a simple example. Suppose you need three tricks, not all four, from the following suit. How can you give yourself the best chance?

To score all four heart tricks you would need to find West with Q-x-x. You would play the king and then finesse the ♠J. When you need only three tricks from the suit, you should start by 'cashing the top cards'. You should play the ace and king and then lead towards the jack on the third round. Why is this better than finessing the jack on the second round? Because you make the required three tricks when East has a doubleton queen. When West holds the queen, there is no need to finesse on the second round. Leading towards the jack on the third round will still give you the three tricks that you require.

This is a more complicated situation:

How should you seek three diamond tricks? If East holds ◊Q-J-x-x(-x), it would suit you to play the king and then finesse the 10 on the second round. If instead East holds ◊Q-x-x-x or ◊J-x-x-x, you would fare better by cashing the ace and king first. You would drop West's doubleton honour on the second round and could then lead towards your 10 on the third round. When the four-card holding lies in the closed hand, it is easily best to cash the king and ace. That's because East might decide to split his honours if his holding included the queen and jack. In any case East is twice as likely to hold Q-x-x-x or J-x-x-x, rather than Q-J-x-x.

Here is a situation that you will often encounter in the trump suit:

♠ A Q 10 6 2

♠ 8 7 5 3

If you needed all five spade tricks, you would finesse the queen on the first round. You would succeed when West held a doubleton king or East held a singleton jack (you could then finesse the 10 on the second round). What if you needed only four spade tricks to make the contract? How would you play the suit then?

Suppose you play the same way and finesse the queen on the first round. If you lose to the king, you will have an agonising dilemma on the second round when you lead towards the remaining A-10-6-2 in dummy and West produces the last low spade. Should you finesse or hope to drop the jack from East? It will be a nasty moment for you.

To avoid any such stress, you should play the ace on the first round of the suit. If East shows out, you can lead twice more towards dummy's remaining honours, still scoring four tricks. Otherwise you will lead towards the queen on the second round. You will make four spade tricks whenever this can be done. Meanwhile you will avoid having to guess whether East started with singleton king or K-J doubleton.

Not many players would have taken the correct line on the next deal. See if you are among the elite!

52 Great Bridge Tips

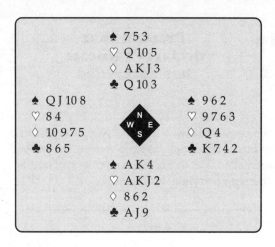

West leads the ♠Q against 6NT. How will you play?

The diamond suit offers a possible safety play. If you need only three diamond tricks, you can start by cashing the ace and king. As we saw a moment ago, you will pick up a doubleton queen with East and can otherwise lead towards the ◊J on the third round. How many diamond tricks do you need for this particular contract? The answer is that you do not know until you have taken the club finesse!

After winning the spade lead, you should cross to dummy with the ♡10 and run the ♣Q. If the finesse wins, continue with a club to the ♣J. When East holds the ♣K you will score three club tricks. That will give you nine top tricks outside the diamond suit. Since three diamond tricks will bring your total to twelve, you can afford to make the safety play in diamonds, cashing the top honours first.

What if the club finesse had lost? You would then have only eight top tricks outside the diamond suit. Needing a full four diamond tricks you would have to find West with ◊Q-x-x.

If you are familiar with squeezes, you may have noticed that you can also succeed when West holds the sole spade guard and ◊Q-x-x-x. You would cash your winners in hearts and clubs and West would have to throw one of his guards (see Tip 33).

W hen declarer takes a finesse that you expect to be repeated, it is often beneficial, as a defender, to pretend that it has succeeded. The technique can prove spectacular when the suit lies in an otherwise entryless dummy.

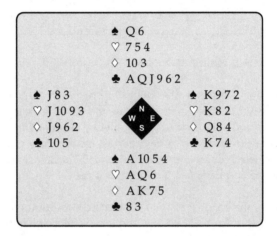

```
                    ♠ Q 6
                    ♡ 7 5 4
                    ◇ 10 3
                    ♣ A Q J 9 6 2
    ♠ J 8 3                        ♠ K 9 7 2
    ♡ J 10 9 3          N          ♡ K 8 2
    ◇ J 9 6 2      W        E      ◇ Q 8 4
    ♣ 10 5             S          ♣ K 7 4
                    ♠ A 10 5 4
                    ♡ A Q 6
                    ◇ A K 7 5
                    ♣ 8 3
```

West, your partner, leads the ♡J against 3NT. You play the king, just in case West has led from A-J-10-x(-x), and declarer wins with the heart ace. How will you defend when declarer's next move is to finesse the ♣Q?

If you win with the ♣K, declarer will score five club tricks and make the contract easily. Instead you should play low, pretending that the finesse has succeeded. Declarer will probably return to his hand with the ◇A and repeat the club finesse. You win with the king and the dummy is dead. Declarer will make only one club trick instead of five.

Many defenders would find that play, because it's basically the same as holding up an ace in dummy's long suit. It would be more difficult here:

♣ A Q J 9 6 2

♣ 10 7 5   ♣ K 4

♣ 8 3

Again when declarer finesses the club queen you must hold up. Provided you do so without apparent thought, declarer is likely to repeat the finesse on the second round.

Another reason to pretend that a finesse has succeeded is to draw declarer into a losing line of play. On the next deal declarer may well waste an entry to dummy if he thinks the first finesse has succeeded.

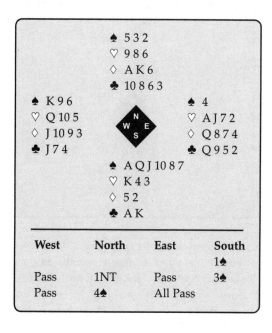

♠ 5 3 2
♡ 9 8 6
♢ A K 6
♣ 10 8 6 3

♠ K 9 6
♡ Q 10 5
♢ J 10 9 3
♣ J 7 4

♠ 4
♡ A J 7 2
♢ Q 8 7 4
♣ Q 9 5 2

♠ A Q J 10 8 7
♡ K 4 3
♢ 5 2
♣ A K

West	North	East	South
			1♠
Pass	1NT	Pass	3♠
Pass	4♠	All Pass	

Suppose you are sitting West and lead the ♢J against South's spade game. Declarer wins in the dummy and leads a trump to the queen. How will you defend?

You can see what will happen if you win with the ♠K. Declarer will win the diamond continuation in dummy and use his last entry to play a heart to the ♡K. With the ♡A onside, he will make the contract. Instead you should allow declarer's ♠Q to win. This can hardly cost, since South's 3♠ rebid showed a six-card suit and you can be almost certain of the spade position. If declarer believes that your partner has the ♠K he will cross to dummy (for the last time) and repeat the spade finesse. It will be a nasty moment for him when East shows out. Not only will he have to lose a trump trick, he will have to concede three heart tricks too and go one down.

To give declarer a further small nudge in the wrong direction, you can follow with the ♠9 when he finesses on the first round. He is then quite likely to place your partner with ♠K-6-4.

We will end this Tip with one more deal where you can deflect declarer from the winning line of play by pretending that a finesse has succeeded. Take the West cards. Would you have managed to fool the declarer?

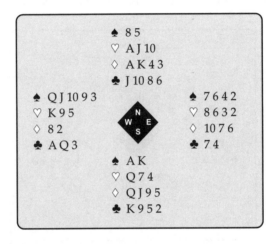

```
                    ♠ 8 5
                    ♡ A J 10
                    ◇ A K 4 3
                    ♣ J 10 8 6
    ♠ Q J 10 9 3              ♠ 7 6 4 2
    ♡ K 9 5          N        ♡ 8 6 3 2
    ◇ 8 2         W     E     ◇ 10 7 6
    ♣ A Q 3          S        ♣ 7 4
                    ♠ A K
                    ♡ Q 7 4
                    ◇ Q J 9 5
                    ♣ K 9 5 2
```

Playing in 3NT, declarer wins your spade lead. With seven tricks on top, it will seem to him that he needs to find either the ♣Q or the ♡K onside. If he takes a losing heart finesse first, the spades will be cleared and he might then go down when the ♣Q was onside. So, declarer will cross to the ◇A and run the ♣J. How do you plan to defend in the West seat?

Suppose you win with the ♣Q and clear the spade suit. Declarer knows that he will go down if he clears the clubs (he will lose at least three spades and two clubs). He will therefore be forced to take the heart finesse and will make the contract when this wins. A better idea is to win the ♣J with the ace, pretending that the finesse against the ♣Q has succeeded! When you clear the spade suit, declarer must decide whether to finesse in clubs again or to finesse in hearts. Since the club finesse has apparently succeeded already, he will surely repeat his finesse in that suit. You will win with the ♣Q and cash three spades to beat the contract.

52 Great Bridge Tips

Tip 23

Develop your main side suit before drawing trumps

W hat is the most common method of planning a suit contract? It's far from the best way but it goes something like this: you win the opening lead, draw trumps, and then sit back in your chair wondering what to do next! On many hands you will get away with this. On some hands, though, you will go down if you draw trumps straight away. This Tip is concerned with hands where you must develop a side suit before drawing trumps.

The most common reason to do this is that dummy has only three trumps and you will need a third-round entry in the trump suit to reach the established cards in the side suit. Many players would go down here:

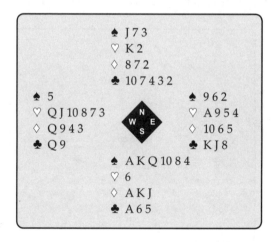

```
                    ♠ J 7 3
                    ♡ K 2
                    ◊ 8 7 2
                    ♣ 10 7 4 3 2
  ♠ 5                              ♠ 9 6 2
  ♡ Q J 10 8 7 3                   ♡ A 9 5 4
  ◊ Q 9 4 3                        ◊ 10 6 5
  ♣ Q 9                            ♣ K J 8
                    ♠ A K Q 10 8 4
                    ♡ 6
                    ◊ A K J
                    ♣ A 6 5
```

West leads the ♡Q against your spade game. How will you play?

You have nine easy tricks and one way to try for a tenth would be to take the diamond finesse. That's only a 50% chance, though, and would fail as the cards lie. A better idea is to try to set up the clubs, hoping for a 3-2 club break. If no luck comes from that direction you can fall back on the diamond finesse, thereby combining two chances instead of relying on just one. How should the play go?

The first point is that you should play low from dummy at Trick 1. There

---

is not one chance in a thousand that West holds the ♡A. If you make the mistake of covering the ♡Q with dummy's king, East will win and perhaps defeat the contract by switching to diamonds. (The defenders would then set up the ◊Q before you had established the clubs.) You ruff the second round of hearts and draw just one round of trumps with the ace. Now you continue with ace and another club. If East wins and fires a diamond through, you will rise with the ace. You then draw a second round of trumps and play another club. There is nothing the defenders can do. You win East's diamond return with the king and cross to the ♠J, drawing East's last trump. You can then take a well deserved diamond discard on one of dummy's established clubs.

Do you see what would go wrong if you drew a second round of trumps before playing on clubs? East could return a third round of trump when he gained the lead, removing dummy's entry before the clubs were set up.

Even when dummy has only two trumps, you may need to use a trump entry in order to set up a long side suit. That's what happens here:

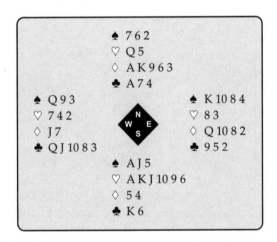

```
              ♠ 7 6 2
              ♡ Q 5
              ◊ A K 9 6 3
              ♣ A 7 4
♠ Q 9 3                      ♠ K 10 8 4
♡ 7 4 2          N           ♡ 8 3
◊ J 7        W     E         ◊ Q 10 8 2
♣ Q J 10 8 3     S           ♣ 9 5 2
              ♠ A J 5
              ♡ A K J 10 9 6
              ◊ 5 4
              ♣ K 6
```

How would you play 6♡ when West leads the ♣Q?

If you had to rely on the spade suit alone, to provide an extra trick, prospects would not be good. You would have to lead twice towards the ♠A-J-5, hoping that East held both the king and queen. Fortunately you have a great chance to set up dummy's diamond suit, thereby providing at least one discard. How should you tackle the play?

You should win the club lead with the king, preserving dummy's ♣A as an entry for later in the play. If you draw three rounds of trumps next, you would waste the entry that dummy's ♡Q represents. You could then set up and enjoy dummy's diamonds only if they broke 3-3. To succeed against a 4-2 diamond break, you must play on diamonds before drawing trumps. Play just the ace of trumps and continue with the two top diamonds. Ruff a diamond with the king, noting the 4-2 break, and return to dummy with the queen of trumps. You can then ruff another diamond with a high trump, setting up dummy's last diamond. After drawing the outstanding trump, you can cross to the ♣A to throw one of your spade losers on the established diamond.

Sometimes you need to repeat a finesse in a side suit in your own hand. You may then have to make full use of the entries to dummy that the trump suit provides. Look at this deal:

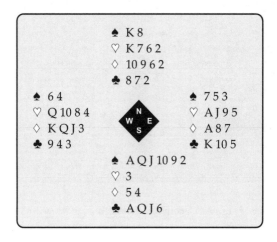

How would you play the spade game when the defenders lead three rounds of diamonds?

Since you will need both the king and eight of trumps as entries, you must ruff the third round of diamonds with the ♠9. Your next move is a heart towards the king, hoping to set up a discard for your fourth club. No luck from that quarter! The king loses to the ace and East returns another heart. You ruff with the ♠10 and lead the ♠2 to dummy's ♠8. A finesse of the club queen wins, you are pleased to see, and you return to dummy with the ♠K. After finessing the ♣J, you can draw East's last trump and play the ♣A. Luck is with you and the suit breaks 3-3. You can claim the remaining tricks.

This deal was another example of combining two chances instead of relying on just one. You needed the ♣K to be onside, yes, but there were two chances to dispose of your fourth club. The first was to find West with the ♡A (you could then throw a club on the ♡K). The second chance was that clubs might break 3-3. To combine both of these chances, you had to make maximum use of dummy's two trump entries.

Even when the dummy has no entries in the trump suit, it can be right to play on a side suit before drawing trumps. Can you think of a situation where this may be necessary? You may need to set up a discard. If instead you play on trumps first, the defenders may win and clear the setting trick. That's the situation here:

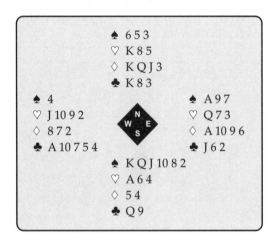

West leads the ♡J against your spade game. How would you play the contract?

Let's see first what will happen to a member of the 'draw trumps first and then make a plan' brigade. He wins with the ♡A and leads the king of trumps. East wins immediately with the ace and plays another heart, won in the dummy. When declarer belatedly sits back and attempts to make a plan, he will find that he has one loser in every suit and there is nothing he can do about it.

After winning the heart lead with the ace (retaining dummy's ♡K as an entry to dummy), you should of course lead a diamond to the king. If this is allowed to win, you continue with the ♢Q. East wins with the ace and clears the heart suit but this places you in dummy. You can discard your heart loser on the ♢J. Now is the time to draw trumps!

Tip 24

With a total of nine trumps bid to the nine-trick level

On many competitive deals your side will have a good fit in one suit and the opponents will have a good fit in another. How high should you compete? A sound general rule is that you should bid to the level dictated by the total number of trumps that you and your partner hold. With 9 trumps between you, compete to the 9-trick level. Strange as it may seem, the total number of trumps is more important than the number of points you may hold. Why is that? Extra high cards will increase the chance of making your own contract, yes, but they will also assist in beating any enemy contract. So, holding an extra ace or king is not necessarily a reason to bid higher (assuming that you are still at the part-score level). You might do better to extract a penalty from the opponents' contract.

Let's look at a typical deal where one side has the spades and the other has the hearts.

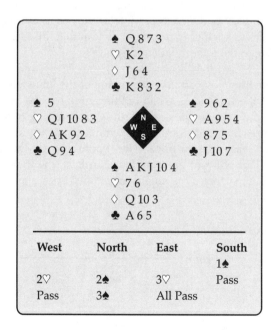

West	North	East	South
			1♠
2♡	2♠	3♡	Pass
Pass	3♠	All Pass	

North-South hold nine spades between them and should therefore be willing to compete to the three-level. How will they fare in 3♠? They will actually go one down, losing two hearts, two diamonds and one club. Does that mean they were wrong to compete so high? Not at all, because East-West would have made their contract of 3♡. At duplicate North-South would lose 50 (or 100 if vulnerable) instead of 140.

You may think that the success or failure of key finesses will have a bearing on the matter. Not necessarily! Suppose that South held the ♡K instead of North. West's contract of 3♡ would then have gone one down (losing two clubs and one trick in each of the other suits). It would still have been worth bidding 3♠, though, because with the ♡K in the South hand, South would have made nine tricks.

The same logic applies when you move a high card from one side to the other. Suppose, in the previous diagram, you swap West's ♣Q with South's ♣5. The East-West contract of 3♡ would now fail even though the heart finesse was right. They would lose one spade, one diamond and three club tricks. Once again, though, it would be worthwhile for North-South to compete to 3♠ because they would make the contract. They would lose only two hearts and two diamonds.

One deal proves nothing and you may suspect that I have chosen it specially to justify the concept of bidding to the level dictated by the total number of trumps. No, the concept of 'total trumps' is one aspect of the Law of Total Tricks – a highly respected dictum that links the number of tricks available to the total number of trumps.

It's time to see how you can take advantage of the knowledge that you should bid to the three-level when holding nine trumps between you. Look back to the previous deal. If North is playing a system where his partner promises five cards for the 1♠ opening, he already knows that his side holds at least nine trumps. He should bid to the three-level immediately. This will put great pressure on East, the fourth player to bid. When your partner's opening is overcalled, you should play this scheme:

After a start of:

West	North	East	South
1♠	?♣	?	

     52 Great Bridge Tips

East can express a spade raise with one of these bids:

2♠	6-10 points and only three-card support
3♣	10+ points and four-card support
3♠	5-9 points and four-card support
4♣/4◇/4♡	Splinter bid, game raise with a side-suit shortage
4♠	5-9 points and five-card support

Following the concept of 'total trumps' you raise to the two-level when you have three-card support and therefore expect your side to hold only eight trumps. With four-card support you jump to the three-level, bidding 3♠ with a fairly weak hand and cue-bidding the opponent's suit when you are stronger. With five-card support, you expect your side to hold at least ten trumps and should therefore jump to the four-level.

(Note that this is the right method to play, even if your system allows you to open on four-card majors. Partner will often hold five cards in his suit, even so. If you play the weak 1NT, an opening of 1♡ or 1♠ nearly always promises either a five-card suit or a balanced hand of 15 or more points. So, when partner has only four cards in his suit, he will have some extra points to assist the contract.)

You may wonder what you do when you have three-card spade support and 11 or more points. One possibility is to start with a negative (take-out) double. You might also respond with a natural and forcing bid of 2◇ or 2♡. In both cases you intend to support spades on the next round.

Test yourself on these three East hands:

(1)	**(2)**	**(3)**
♠ K J 3	♠ A 10 7 6	♠ Q J 8 3
♡ A 9 8 2	♡ J 5	♡ A 10 7 6
◇ J 10 8 4	◇ 10 8 7 6 2	◇ K J 5
♣ 7 6	♣ 9 3	♣ 8 4

West	North	East	South
1♠	2◇	?	

You have only three-card trump support on (1) and should indicate this with a raise to 2♠. You are near the top end of the 6-10 point range for this response. You have several points fewer on hand (2) but precious four-card trump support. Jump to 3♠ to show a weakish hand with four trumps. This will make life very awkward for South. Indeed, that is the main purpose of such a response. If you bid 3♠ on the second hand, you obviously can't make the same response on (3), where you have four-card support and want to invite a game if partner has anything to spare for his opening bid. You cue-bid 3◊, to show exactly this type of hand. If partner has a minimum and rebids just 3♠, you will pass on this occasion.

The same principle applies when an opponent has doubled your partner's opening bid for take-out. After this start to the auction:

West	North	East	South
1♠	Dbl	?	

East can express a hand with spade support using one of these bids:

2♠	6-10 points and only three-card support
2NT	10+ points and four-card support
3♠	5-9 points and four-card support
4♣/4◊/4♡	Splinter bid, game raise with a side-suit shortage
4♠	5-9 points and five-card support

When you hold three-card support and more than 10 points, as responder, you do best to start with a redouble, intending to show your spade support on the next round. Once again, you could also make a splinter bid, such as 4♣, to show a sound raise to game including at most one card in the suit that you bid.

There is one other important situation where you should raise your partner immediately to the three-level when you hold four-card support – when your partner has overcalled. Suppose the bidding starts like this:

West	North	East	South
1♡	1♠	Pass	?

With spade support, you should bid as follows:

2♠	6-10 points and only three-card support
2♡	10+ points and four-card support
3♠	5-9 points and four-card support
4♠	5-9 points and five-card support

Tip
25

Force a defender to give you a ruff-and-discard

In Tip 19, we looked at elimination play — a very common technique where you eliminate one or more side suits and then throw an opponent on lead, forcing him to open a new suit. The present Tip deals with a slightly different situation, where you cannot completely eliminate one of the side suits but may be able to remove the cards of one particular defender. You can then throw him on lead, forcing him to give you a ruff-and-discard. It's not easy to visualize, perhaps, so let's look at a straightforward example of this technique.

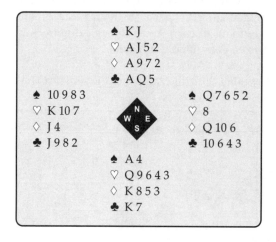

West leads the ♠10 against 6♡. How will you tackle the play?

You win the spade lead with the ace and lead a trump to the jack. If a singleton ♡10 appears from East, your Q-9 in the suit will be good for a finesse against West's ♡K. As it is, only the ♡8 appears from East. You therefore continue with the ace of hearts, discovering that you have a loser in the suit. Since there is an apparent loser in diamonds, however the diamonds lie, you may think that defeat is imminent.

Not at all! You play the ◊K and continue with a low diamond towards the ace. (You are following Tip 17, leading towards an honour to avoid a possible ruff.) You then play the remaining spade honour followed by three rounds of clubs, on which you throw a diamond loser. These cards remain:

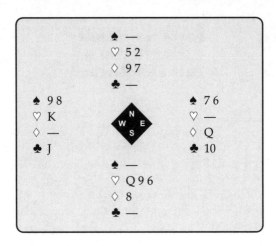

You now play a trump, throwing West on lead. Since West does not hold the outstanding diamond, he has to return one or other black suit, conceding a ruff-and-discard. You ruff with dummy's last trump and throw the ◊8 from your hand. Slam made!

Here a slightly more difficult example of the same technique:

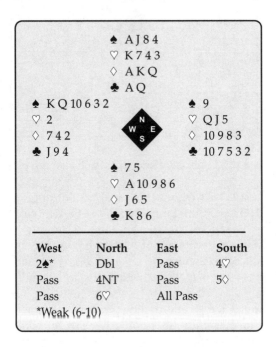

West	North	East	South
2♠*	Dbl	Pass	4♡
Pass	4NT	Pass	5◊
Pass	6♡	All Pass	
*Weak (6-10)			

How would you play 6♡ when West leads the ♠K?

Suppose you win with the ♠A and play two top trumps, discovering that you have a loser there. If you can cash all your own minor-suit cards, you will be able to throw East in with a trump and he will have to give you a ruff-and-discard. (West's weak two tells you that East started with one spade.) Unfortunately, the club suit is blocked. After playing the ace and queen of clubs, you will have no entry to the South hand, to cash the ♣K.

You have to play the ♣A-Q before playing the second round of trumps to your ace. You can then cash the ♣K, followed by three diamonds. East is doomed. You throw him in with a trump and he has to give you a ruff-and-discard, which allows you to throw your spade loser.

Here is one more example where you need to display some foresight.

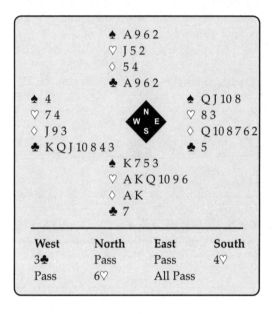

	♠ A 9 6 2		
	♡ J 5 2		
	◊ 5 4		
	♣ A 9 6 2		

♠ 4		♠ Q J 10 8
♡ 7 4		♡ 8 3
◊ J 9 3		◊ Q 10 8 7 6 2
♣ K Q J 10 8 4 3		♣ 5

	♠ K 7 5 3	
	♡ A K Q 10 9 6	
	◊ A K	
	♣ 7	

West	North	East	South
3♣	Pass	Pass	4♡
Pass	6♡	All Pass	

West leads the ♣K against your small slam. How will you play it?

All will be well if spades are 3-2. If not, you will need to throw West in to give you a ruff-and-discard. Win the club lead and ruff a club at Trick 2! Play the ace and jack of trumps and ruff another club. Cash the top diamonds followed by the king and ace of spades. When spades do prove to be 4-1, lead dummy's last club and throw a spade loser. West will have to win and, yes, give you a ruff-and-discard. Away goes your last spade and you make the slam.

Tip 26

Against a suit contract do not lead an unsupported ace

When you are on lead against a no-trump contract, it is often right to lead from a suit headed by the ace. Suppose you hold ♠A-J-8-5-2, for example. The fourth-best spade is an excellent lead! You don't mind giving away an early trick. If you can establish the suit, you may be able to beat the contract.

Now suppose you are on lead against a suit contract. Should you lead from a suit headed by the ace? Unless you also hold the king, the answer is nearly always: no! Certainly you should not lead a low card from such a suit. If you feel you must lead the suit, you should lead the ace.

Let's see how leading an unsupported ace can cost a trick:

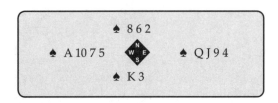

What is the effect of leading the ♠A here? You set up a trick for declarer's king. If you lead some different suit, he will eventually lead towards the king and fail to make a trick from the suit.

If you lead the ♡A here, declarer will make an undeserved trick with the ♡Q. Lead some other suit and he cannot score a heart trick.

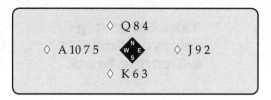

♢ Q 8 4

♢ A 10 7 5   ♢ J 9 2

♢ K 6 3

Lead the ♢A and declarer scores tricks with both the king and the queen.

There are many more examples, but you have the picture by now. Think of your ace as a fishing net. You are meant to catch something with it – preferably a juicy king-fish or a queen-fish. If you simply lead the card, you will end with a net full of tiddlers!

Suppose you are West with these cards:

♠ 9 7 2	**West**	**North**	**East**	**South**
♡ A 10 3	1♢	Pass	1♡	1♠
♢ K Q 7 6 2	2♡	2♠	All Pass	
♣ K 5				

What will you lead? Partner has bid hearts, yes, and many players would decide to 'lead partner's suit', starting with the ♡A. It is not a good lead! A one-level response does not promise a good suit, it merely shows at least 6 points and least four hearts. Even if partner holds ♡K-x-x-x, you may find that leading the ♡A sets up declarer's ♡Q. So, look elsewhere. Either lead the ♢K or play safe with a trump lead.

These are the only situations where you should consider leading an ace:

- The opponents have bid three suits, avoided playing in 3NT and ended in five of a minor. It is reasonable to lead the ace of the unbid suit, expecting partner to hold the king.

- On lead against a small slam, you have a potential trick in one of declarer's suits (perhaps trumps) and want to cash an ace in a different suit in case declarer can discard his losers there.

- You expect partner to be strong in the suit where you hold the ace. He has made an overcall in the suit, for example.

Otherwise choose a lead from some other suit.

Tip

27

Take early steps to overcome a 4-1 trump break

You play two rounds of trumps and discover that the defenders' trumps are breaking 4-1. What now? You may find that it is too late to do anything about it! On many deals you must foresee the possibility and take precautions before the bad news comes to light.

The simplest technique in this area is a safety play in the trump suit alone. Even though it is a relatively easy to perform, you can be sure that several players at your local club would go down on the following deal. See how you fare yourself. No-one is watching!

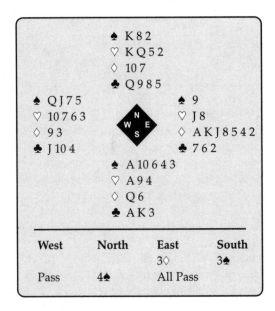

	♠ K 8 2	
	♡ K Q 5 2	
	◊ 10 7	
	♣ Q 9 8 5	

♠ Q J 7 5		♠ 9
♡ 10 7 6 3		♡ J 8
◊ 9 3		◊ A K J 8 5 4 2
♣ J 10 4		♣ 7 6 2

	♠ A 10 6 4 3
	♡ A 9 4
	◊ Q 6
	♣ A K 3

West	North	East	South
		3◊	3♠
Pass	4♠	All Pass	

West leads the ◊9 against your spade game. East cashes two winners in the suit, all following, and switches to a club. How will you play?

All depends on restricting your trump losers to one. What is the best way to play the suit? If there had been no bidding by the opponents, you would cash the ♠K first and lead towards the South hand, planning to put in the 10 unless an honour appeared from East. That would be best because you could pick up any four-card holding (even Q-J-9-x) in the East hand.

On the present deal East has seven diamonds to his partner's two. That means that West is much more likely to hold four spades than East. Also, most players are unwilling to open a minor-suit pre-empt when they hold a four-card major. For those two reasons, you should concentrate on picking up four trumps in the West hand. You can do this whenever East holds a singleton queen, jack or 9. You cash the ace on the first round, the 9 appearing from East and then lead towards dummy, planning to insert the 8. If West chooses to split his honours, you will win with the king and return the ♠8 to force out West's remaining honour.

On the next deal the defenders attack your long trump holding.

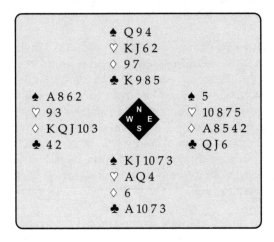

```
            ♠ Q 9 4
            ♡ K J 6 2
            ◇ 9 7
            ♣ K 9 8 5
♠ A 8 6 2                    ♠ 5
♡ 9 3          N            ♡ 10 8 7 5
◇ K Q J 10 3  W   E         ◇ A 8 5 4 2
♣ 4 2             S         ♣ Q J 6
            ♠ K J 10 7 3
            ♡ A Q 4
            ◇ 6
            ♣ A 10 7 3
```

Holding four trumps to the ace, always a precious asset in defence, West leads the king of diamonds. His aim is to attack your long trump holding, thereby promoting the value of his own trumps. Pleased to see the diamond king win, West continues with the queen of diamonds. How will you play the contract?

Let's see first what will happen if you ruff the second diamond. You play a trump to the queen and continue with a second round of trumps. Bad news arrives when East shows out, throwing a diamond. Even worse news arrives when West allows the second round of trumps to win. Do you see the problem now? This is the remaining position in the trump suit:

♠ 9

♠ A 8   ♠ —

♠ J 10

If you play a third round of trumps, West will win and play another diamond to force your last trump. You will have lost trump control. West will be able to ruff in at some stage and cash his remaining diamonds. What will happen if you turn to the side suits, instead of playing a third round of trumps. That's no good either. West will score a ruff with his ♠8, along with the trump ace and a further loser in the club suit. One down!

Do you see how to overcome a 4-1 trump break? At Trick 2 you should discard a club loser instead of ruffing. A third round of diamonds will not damage you now because you can take the ruff in dummy – in the short trump holding. Whatever else West tries, you will be able to win and knock out the ace of trumps. Since you have one more trump than West, he cannot hurt you by holding up the trump ace for two rounds and playing a further diamond. You will have preserved trump control. That's an important technique to remember, then. You discard one or more losers from the long-trump hand, waiting for the moment when the short-trump hand can ruff.

When you can afford to lose a trump trick, it sometimes makes good sense to duck a round of trumps early in the play, while you still have trumps in the dummy to protect you against an attack in the defenders' best suit. This deal illustrates the technique:

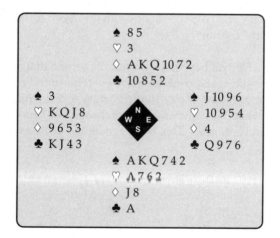

♠ 8 5
♥ 3
♦ A K Q 10 7 2
♣ 10 8 5 2

♠ 3   ♠ J 10 9 6
♥ K Q J 8   ♥ 10 9 5 4
♦ 9 6 5 3   ♦ 4
♣ K J 4 3   ♣ Q 9 7 6

♠ A K Q 7 4 2
♥ A 7 6 2
♦ J 8
♣ A

West leads the ♡K against 6♠ and you win with the ace. Thirteen tricks will be easy if trumps break 3-2. (Thirteen tricks would have been easy in diamonds, even when spades do break 4-1. Still, it's too late to worry about the bidding.) Your task is to ensure that you make twelve tricks in spades.

You win the heart lead with the ace and play the ace of trumps. Do you? If that is your first move, you will go down! The king of trumps will reveal the 4-1 break and the defenders will be able to cash a heart or two when East gains the lead with his ♠J.

What else can you try? Perhaps you should ruff a couple of hearts in dummy? Let's see what happens if you try that. You win the heart lead, ruff a heart, cross to the ♣A and ruff another heart. You return to your hand with the ◇J (or a club ruff) and play the ace and king of trumps, discovering the 4-1 break. You draw a third round of trumps and turn to the diamond suit, hoping to discard your last heart. Not today! East will ruff the second round of diamonds and you will be one down.

There is only one safe line. You must lead a low trump from your hand at Trick 2! East wins his trump trick at a moment that is convenient to you. There is still a trump in dummy, so he cannot profit by a heart return. Whatever else he tries, you will win, draw trumps and run the diamonds. So, that's another technique to add to your repertoire. To guard against a 4-1 break, give up a trump trick when the defenders can do you no damage.

Tip
28

Use the
Rule of 15
in fourth position

The auction starts with three passes and you have to decide whether to open in the fourth seat. When your hand is a minimum, there is always a risk that the opponents will contest the bidding and finish with a plus score when you might have passed the deal out. How can you decide? One of the most important factors is the spade suit. The side that owns the senior suit will have the best chance of winning the auction. You should therefore be wary of opening light in the fourth seat when you are short of spades. Look at this typical deal:

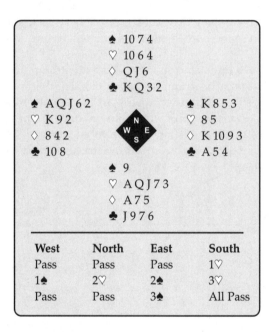

West	North	East	South
Pass	Pass	Pass	1♡
1♠	2♡	2♠	3♡
Pass	Pass	3♠	All Pass

West ends in 3♠ and makes the contract, giving you a minus score. Of course, it's just one layout from the billions that are possible, but it illustrates the risk of opening light in the fourth seat when you are short in spades. Use this guideline, the Rule of 15, to decide whether you should open: *in the fourth seat open the bidding when the total of your points and the number of spades is 15 or more.* Here South had 12 points and 1 spade – a total of just 13. This was a warning that he should not have opened the bidding.

Tip
29

Duck a trick into the safe hand

When you will have to lose a trick in order to establish a suit, or may have to if it breaks badly, you should try to duck a trick into the safe hand. You give the lead to the defender who cannot do you any damage. The situation arises commonly when you are missing four trumps to the queen. Look at this deal:

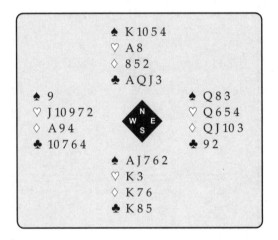

```
                  ♠ K 10 5 4
                  ♡ A 8
                  ◇ 8 5 2
                  ♣ A Q J 3
   ♠ 9                             ♠ Q 8 3
   ♡ J 10 9 7 2        N           ♡ Q 6 5 4
   ◇ A 9 4          W     E        ◇ Q J 10 3
   ♣ 10 7 6 4          S           ♣ 9 2
                  ♠ A J 7 6 2
                  ♡ K 3
                  ◇ K 7 6
                  ♣ K 8 5
```

West leads the ♡J against 4♠. How would you plan the play?

With nine cards in the trump suit, you would normally follow the 'Eight Ever, Nine Never' guideline and play to drop the queen in two rounds. Do you see why that is wrong here? Suppose you win the heart lead with the king and cash the king and ace of trumps, West showing out on the second round. You will now have to turn to the club suit, hoping that East will follow three times. No, he will ruff the third round of clubs and switch to a deadly ◇Q. The defenders will soon have three diamond tricks before them and that will be one down.

If you needed to bring in the trump suit without loss, the percentage play would indeed be to play the ace and king. On this particular deal, however, you can afford to lose a trick in trumps. (You will still then score at least four spades, two hearts and four clubs.) What you cannot afford to do is to lose a trump trick to East, the danger hand.

So, you should win the heart lead with the king, cross to the ♠K and finesse the ♠J. If the finesse wins, you will make the contract. If the finesse loses, you will make the contract. What could be a better proposition than that? You don't mind finessing into a doubleton queen with West because the diamonds are safe from attack with West on lead. Once the trumps are drawn, you can play four rounds of clubs and discard one of your diamonds.

Here is another deal on the same theme:

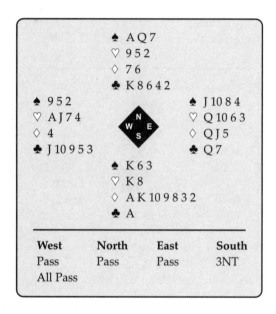

	♠ A Q 7	
	♡ 9 5 2	
	◇ 7 6	
	♣ K 8 6 4 2	
♠ 9 5 2		♠ J 10 8 4
♡ A J 7 4		♡ Q 10 6 3
◇ 4		◇ Q J 5
♣ J 10 9 5 3		♣ Q 7
	♠ K 6 3	
	♡ K 8	
	◇ A K 10 9 8 3 2	
	♣ A	

West	North	East	South
Pass	Pass	Pass	3NT
All Pass			

When you pay good money for a bridge book you expect to see better bidding than that? I can only agree but the deal is from actual play and that is how the bidding went. How would you play 3NT when West leads the ♣J?

Declarer won the club lead with the bare ace and now needed to set up the diamond suit. Since six diamond tricks would be more than enough for the contract, he could afford to lose a trick in the suit. What he could not afford was to let East gain the lead in diamonds. A heart switch would then threaten the contract. At Trick 2, declarer crossed to dummy with the ♠Q. He then led a diamond towards his hand. East played the ◇5 and declarer covered with the ◇10, fully expecting to lose the trick. If that were to happen the remainder of the diamond suit would be good and West, the safe hand, would be on lead. As it happened, the ◇10 won the trick and declarer ended with no fewer than twelve tricks.

If East had split his honours on the first round of diamonds, declarer would have won with the ace and re-entered dummy in spades to finesse the ◊10. Make sure you have understood the point of the play. It was not that you 'wanted to pick up East's Q-J-x in diamonds'. What you were aiming to do was to set up the diamond suit without allowing East on lead. Unless diamonds were 4-0, one way or another, you could guarantee the contract.

Sometimes you can duck a trick to the defender who sits underneath your strong holding in a suit. That's what happens here.

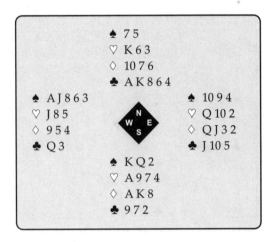

West leads the ♣6 against 3NT and East plays the ♣9. You win the trick and note that East is now the 'danger hand', since a spade through your remaining honour may spell defeat. You need to set up dummy's clubs without the danger hand gaining the lead. How can this be done?

Suppose you play ace, king and another club. If West had started with three cards in the suit, all would be well. He would have to win the third round and you would be safe. When East has three clubs, as in the diagram, you would go down. He would win the third round of clubs and the defenders would score four spade tricks.

When West has only two clubs, you will need him to hold the ♣Q in order to make the contract. Lead a club towards the dummy. If West should happen to play the queen, you will duck and leave the safe hand on lead. It is more likely that West will play low on the first round. You win with dummy's ♣A and return to the South hand to lead another club towards dummy. The queen appears from West and you duck, leaving the safe hand on lead. Nine tricks are yours.

Tip

30

**Avoid being endplayed
when declarer plays
the last suit**

Suppose declarer plays a deal on elimination lines, drawing trumps and eliminating two side suits. As a defender, you must avoid being endplayed when declarer plays the last suit. Look at this deal:

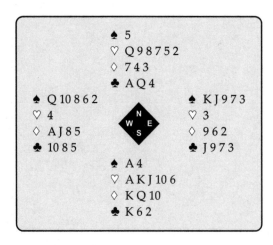

Sitting West, you lead the ♣6 against a small slam in hearts, declarer winning East's king with the ace. He draws trumps, ruffs a spade and plays three rounds of clubs, ending in the dummy. These cards remain:

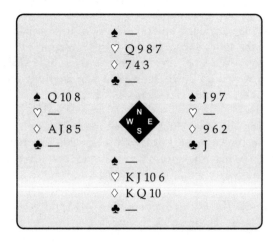

Declarer now leads a diamond from dummy and plays the king. What should you do?

If you win the trick with the ace, which may seem the natural thing to do, you will give away the contract. You will have no safe return. A diamond will be into South's Q-10 tenace and a spade will concede a ruff-and-discard. To beat the contract, you must allow South's ◊K to win. Declarer will then have to play the next round of diamonds himself and you will score two tricks with the ace and jack.

'How can I tell that?' you may be thinking. 'How do I know that South didn't start with king doubleton in the suit? It would be fatal to hold up the ace then.'

The only way to defend well in this situation, and countless other similar positions, is for the defenders to play count signals so that they can each determine the shape of declarer's hand. Here, for example, East will play the ◊2 on the first round of the suit. A low card shows an odd number of cards in diamonds. In the context of the present deal East must hold three diamonds, which leaves three diamonds for South. You can therefore be certain that you should not win the first round. South has two diamonds left, so your ace and jack will both score tricks when declarer eventually plays on diamonds again.

Here is a similar deal. Would you have defended accurately, as West?

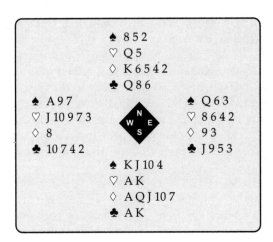

```
                      ♠ 8 5 2
                      ♡ Q 5
                      ◊ K 6 5 4 2
                      ♣ Q 8 6
    ♠ A 9 7                          ♠ Q 6 3
    ♡ J 10 9 7 3          N          ♡ 8 6 4 2
    ◊ 8              W         E      ◊ 9 3
    ♣ 10 7 4 2           S          ♣ J 9 5 3
                      ♠ K J 10 4
                      ♡ A K
                      ◊ A Q J 10 7
                      ♣ A K
```

You lead the ♡J against a small slam in diamonds. Declarer wins in his hand and draws trumps with the ace and queen. Annoyingly for him there is only one entry to dummy in the trump suit, so he cannot take the spade finesse twice. He cashes his remaining winners in hearts and clubs and crosses to dummy with the trump king. One spade can be thrown on the ♣Q and these cards will remain:

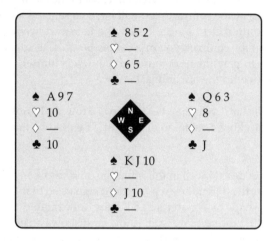

```
                    ♠ 8 5 2
                    ♡ —
                    ◇ 6 5
                    ♣ —
   ♠ A 9 7                          ♠ Q 6 3
   ♡ 10            N                ♡ 8
   ◇ —          W     E             ◇ —
   ♣ 10            S                ♣ J
                    ♠ K J 10
                    ♡ —
                    ◇ J 10
                    ♣ —
```

Hoping for the best, declarer plays a low spade to the jack. If you win with the ace you will be endplayed, forced to return a spade into the K-10 tenace or to concede a ruff-and-discard. The winning defence is to allow South's ♠J to hold. With no entry available to the dummy, declarer will have to lead spades from his own hand. You and your partner will then score two tricks in the suit.

'Yes, yes, that's very clever,' you may be thinking, 'but how can I know that I must defend in that way?'

First of all you must have studied the pips in the trump suit. You must be aware that declarer has no further entry to dummy. Secondly you must have counted declarer's hand and discovered that declarer started with four cards in the spade suit and therefore still had two spades remaining. (If declarer had only one spade remaining, you would have to win the first spade and hope that declarer was missing the ace and king of spades!)

How do you know how many spades South was dealt? Perhaps he bid the suit during the auction. In the absence of any such information, the defenders have to count declarer's hand. He has shown up with five trumps and two clubs. Presumably he held only two hearts in each hand, since the king and the queen were played on the same trick. (East will also have given a count signal in hearts, playing high-low to show an even number of cards.) South's shape must therefore be 4-2-5-2 and it is safe to duck the first spade.

We will end with a different type of end position where, as a defender, you start with a doubleton honour in the key suit. If you play low on the first round, you may be endplayed with the bare honour on the second round and will then have to concede a ruff-and-discard. By playing the honour on the first round of the suit you can avoid this fate.

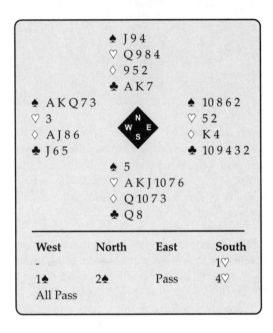

	♠ J 9 4		
	♡ Q 9 8 4		
	◇ 9 5 2		
	♣ A K 7		

♠ A K Q 7 3   ♠ 10 8 6 2
♡ 3   ♡ 5 2
◇ A J 8 6   ◇ K 4
♣ J 6 5   ♣ 10 9 4 3 2

	♠ 5		
	♡ A K J 10 7 6		
	◇ Q 10 7 3		
	♣ Q 8		

West	North	East	South
-			1♡
1♠	2♠	Pass	4♡
All Pass			

North's 2♠ cue-bid shows at least a sound raise in hearts (see Tip 24) and South bids game in the suit. This time you are sitting East. Your partner leads a top spade against South's heart game. A low diamond switch would work brilliantly now but, not being a magician, West continues with a second top spade.

Declarer ruffs and draws trumps. He then ruffs dummy's last spade and plays three rounds of clubs, discarding a diamond from his hand. These cards remain:

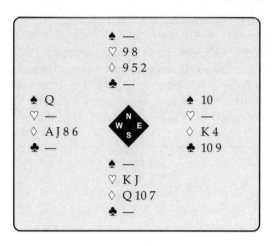

The key moment has arrived. Declarer leads a low diamond from dummy and all depends on your next move. Suppose you play the ◇4. (Either you are asleep or you have not read Chapter 30 of a well-known bridge book.) West will win declarer's ◇10 with the jack and exit with a low diamond. You win with the bare king and... oh no! ... will then have to give declarer a ruff-and-discard.

If you stop to think, it should be obvious that this will be your fate if you leave yourself with the bare king of diamonds. (You know from the fall of the cards that declarer has trumps left in both hands and no cards remaining in either black suit.) You should therefore play the king on the first round of diamonds. The king wins the trick and you can then lead a second round of diamonds through declarer's queen, giving the defenders a total of three diamond tricks to go with the spade trick

Tip
31

Count the other suits before making the key decision

I t often happens that you can tell, after a glance at your own hand and the dummy, that 'everything will depend on guessing the diamonds correctly'. Perhaps you are missing the ◊Q and will need to guess which defender holds that card. Don't be in any hurry to take such a decision. By playing on the other suits first you may uncover valuable information about the distribution of the defenders' hands, even when this does not seem very likely. Look at this typical deal:

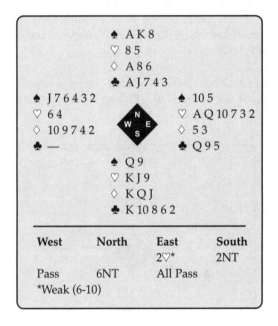

West	North	East	South
		2♡*	2NT
Pass	6NT	All Pass	
*Weak (6-10)			

West leads the ♡6, East playing the ♡10. How will you play the slam?

When the club suit is breaking 3-0, one way or another, you will need to guess which defender holds the ♣Q. If the contract was 6♣ instead of 6NT, you would need to make this guess in the club suit immediately. Which club honour would you play first in that case? Since you expect East to hold six hearts to West's two, you would perhaps judge that West was more likely to hold the longer clubs. In that case you would cash the ♣K on the first round and go one down.

Tip 31   93

In 6NT you do not need to play the club suit straight away. Your best strategy is to play on the other suits before making your final decision in clubs. So, you cash three rounds of spades and are interested to see that East has only two cards in the suit. Next you play three rounds of diamonds. Although you had no reason to expect to receive such clear-cut information, East shows out on the third round of diamonds too! You now have an almost certain count of the East hand. He appears to be 2-6-2-3. You therefore play a low club towards the dummy. West shows out, as you expected, and you rise with the ace. You finesse against East's ♣Q on the second round and make the small slam.

It was somewhat unusual that you were able to obtain a complete count on the hand. Let's see what would happen if the cards lay differently. Suppose when you played on spades and diamonds, East followed to two spades and all three diamonds. Since 2-6-3-3 shape would give East a total of 14 cards, it would then be impossible for him to hold three clubs! You would cash the ♣K on the first round of clubs, knowing that West could not possibly show out.

Let's look at a similar deal where declarer cannot obtain a sufficient count to 'know' that he is guessing right. He can tell enough to be sure that the odds are greatly in his favour.

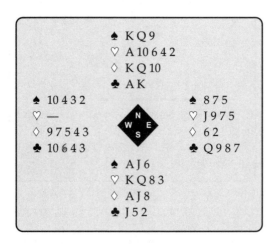

West leads a safe ◊7 against your contract of 7NT. How would you play?

You will have thirteen tricks on top unless the hearts break 4-0, one way or another. You can catch J-9-7-5 on either side, provided you cash an honour from the right hand on the first round of hearts. As on the previous deal, there is nothing to be gained by taking an immediate view in the heart suit. You should seek extra information by cashing three rounds of both spades and diamonds.

What information comes to light? Both defenders follow to three rounds of spades – nothing much learnt there. When you play on diamonds, West has five cards in the suit and East has two. This three-card discrepancy makes East much more likely than West to hold four hearts. For East to be void in hearts, his shape would have to be 4-0-2-7 or 3-0-2-8. In fact it is fourteen times more likely that West is void in hearts! You should therefore play a low heart towards the ace on the first round. You are delighted to see that your detective work has yielded a big dividend. West does indeed show out. You lead a heart towards the ♡K-Q-8 and East splits his J-9, forcing the queen. You cross to the ♣K and finesse the ♡8. After cashing the ♡K, you return to dummy with the ♣A and score the fifth trick in hearts. Grand slam made! As you see, you needed the two club entries to pick up the heart suit when East held all four cards there.

Sometimes the count you obtain will provide only a small advantage in the final guess. Suppose everything depends on guessing this diamond suit:

Three tricks remain and you need to guess which defender holds the ◊Q. You know from playing off the other three suits that West started with four diamonds (he has discarded one) and East started with three. Which defender should you play for the diamond queen?

Since West started with four of the defenders' seven diamonds, he is a 4-to-3 favourite to hold the missing queen. You should therefore finesse dummy's ◊J. Four times out of every seven, the finesse will succeed.

Tip
32

Double to tell
your partner
what to lead

How often does partner lead the suit that you want? Half the time, if you're lucky? Sometimes you can influence his decision by doubling an opponent's artificial bid and that is the subject of this Tip.

There are several situations where a lead-directing double is possible. One is when the opponents have used some form of Blackwood and the artificial response is in the suit that you want to be led. If it is, you can double to tell partner that you are strong in the suit. Here is a typical deal:

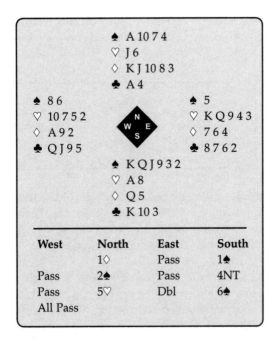

	♠ A 10 7 4		
	♡ J 6		
	◇ K J 10 8 3		
	♣ A 4		

♠ 8 6		♠ 5
♡ 10 7 5 2		♡ K Q 9 4 3
◇ A 9 2		◇ 7 6 4
♣ Q J 9 5		♣ 8 7 6 2

	♠ K Q J 9 3 2
	♡ A 8
	◇ Q 5
	♣ K 10 3

West	North	East	South
	1◇	Pass	1♠
Pass	2♠	Pass	4NT
Pass	5♡	Dbl	6♠
All Pass			

West responds 5♡ to the Blackwood enquiry, showing two aces. This is no time to be asleep in the East seat! With a solid king-queen holding in hearts you should double the artificial 5♡ response to suggest a good opening lead.

South bids 6♠, regardless, but a heart lead defeats the slam. It sets up a heart trick before declarer can establish dummy's diamond suit. Declarer has little option but to win the heart lead, draw trumps and play on diamonds. When West takes the ◊A he plays another heart and that is one down. Without the lead-directing double, West would probably have led the ♣Q. Declarer could then draw trumps, set up the diamond suit and claim the contract.

When you are on lead against a slam contract you must sometimes take note of the fact that partner did not made a lead-directing double of a Blackwood response. Suppose you are sitting West here:

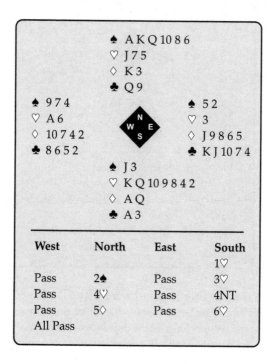

	♠ A K Q 10 8 6		
	♡ J 7 5		
	◊ K 3		
	♣ Q 9		
♠ 9 7 4			♠ 5 2
♡ A 6			♡ 3
◊ 10 7 4 2			◊ J 9 8 6 5
♣ 8 6 5 2			♣ K J 10 7 4
	♠ J 3		
	♡ K Q 10 9 8 4 2		
	◊ A Q		
	♣ A 3		

West	North	East	South
			1♡
Pass	2♠	Pass	3♡
Pass	4♡	Pass	4NT
Pass	5◊	Pass	6♡
All Pass			

After such an auction you will usually lead one of the unbid suits, diamonds or clubs. Here you have nothing special in these suits yourself. Think this way: 'if partner had something good in diamonds, he might have doubled 5◊'. It is more likely that partner has a strong holding in clubs and that is the suit you should lead, other things being equal.

On the layout shown, a club lead is the only one to beat the slam. Dummy's ♣Q is covered by the king and ace. Declarer's only chance is to play three rounds of spades, hoping that the defender with the doubleton spade has no trumps (or a singleton ace of trumps). When

East ruffs the third spade with the ♡3 the slam tumbles to defeat.

The opponents will often use control-showing cue-bids on their way to a slam. You or your partner may then have an opportunity to indicate a lead. Since a cue-bid will often show the ace of the suit bid, you can double with as little as the king sitting over it.

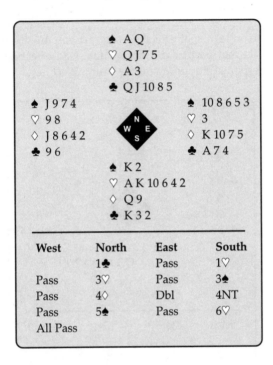

	♠ A Q		
	♡ Q J 7 5		
	◇ A 3		
	♣ Q J 10 8 5		

♠ J 9 7 4   ♠ 10 8 6 5 3
♡ 9 8   ♡ 3
◇ J 8 6 4 2   ◇ K 10 7 5
♣ 9 6   ♣ A 7 4

     ♠ K 2
     ♡ A K 10 6 4 2
     ◇ Q 9
     ♣ K 3 2

West	North	East	South
	1♣	Pass	1♡
Pass	3♡	Pass	3♠
Pass	4◇	Dbl	4NT
Pass	5♣	Pass	6♡
All Pass			

Hearts are agreed as trumps and both 3♠ and 4◇ are control-showing cue-bids. They show either the ace or king of the suit bid and suggest interest in a slam. When East hears that North holds the ◇A he doubles for a diamond opening lead. The opponents persevere regardless and reach a small slam, swiftly dispatched when West heeds his partner's advice and leads a diamond.

Suppose the hands and the auction had been quite different and North had made a Blackwood response of 5◇ (instead of cue-bidding diamonds). There would be much less reason to double because East would not know who held the diamond ace. If it was South, there would be no reason to request a diamond lead. Dummy might hold ◇Q-10-x opposite declarer's ◇A-x, for example, and a diamond lead would give him a chance to avoid a loser there.

     52 Great Bridge Tips

Even at a low level of bidding there are several situations where the opponents use a bid in a defender's suit, usually to show strength. Every time they do this, they give you a chance to make a lead-directing double. Look at this start to an auction:

West	North	East	South
			1♡
1♠	2♠	?	

Your partner has overcalled in spades and North has made a cuebid in spades to show that he has a sound raise to at least the three-level in hearts (3♡ instead would have shown a pre-emptive raise, see Tip 24). Suppose, sitting East, you hold ♠A-x and only 5 or 6 points. You are not worth a bid of any sort but you can double to suggest a spade lead. Partner will expect you to hold a doubleton honour for this bid because if you held ♠A-x-x you would probably have raised the spades.

Once again, partner will take note of the occasions where you have not made a lead-directing double of the third player's cue-bid. In that case he will be wary of leading away from such as K-J-x-x-x in the spade suit and will choose some different opening lead.

Finally, your opponents are likely to use 'fourth suit forcing' a couple of times a session. Be alert for the chance to double the artificial fourth-suit bid:

West	North	East	South
			1♡
Pass	1♠	Pass	2♣
Pass	2◊	?	

You're sitting there with ◊K-Q-10-x-x? Double!

Tip 33

Leave the play of the 4-3 suit until last

Suppose you are in 3NT with eight tricks on top and a possible ninth trick to come from a suit where you hold K-x-x in the dummy and A-Q-x-x in your hand. Should you play on this suit immediately? No, you should leave it until last. For all you know, one of the defenders may elect to discard from a four-card holding. We will look first at a deal where a defender has to guess what to keep.

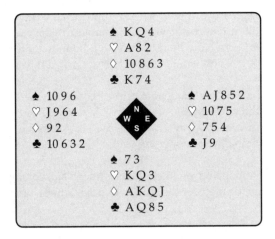

West leads the ♠10 against 6NT, covered by the king and ace, and East returns a spade to dummy's queen. How will you play the contract?

You have eleven tricks on top and the only apparent chance of a twelfth is that the clubs will break 3-3. Suppose no-one gave you a book of Bridge Tips for your birthday and you play for this chance immediately. East will show out on the third round of clubs and you will go one down.

A much better idea is to play four rounds of diamonds first. West will have to find two discards. He throws his last spade on the third diamond but what should he throw on the fourth diamond? It is a complete guess! If you have four hearts, he needs to throw a club and keep four hearts. If instead you hold four clubs, he needs to throw a heart and keep four clubs. Half the time he will guess wrongly and you will make the slam!

It is not only a question of a defender misguessing which cards to keep. Sometimes he will be left with no safe discard and will be forced to give you an extra trick. That's what happens here:

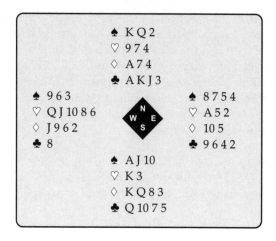

West leads the ♡Q against 6NT. East wins with the ♡A and returns the ♡5. How will you play the slam?

With eleven top tricks it may seem that the only chance is a 3-3 diamond break. There is no point whatsoever in playing the diamond suit immediately. Always delay playing on such a suit until the last moment. Here you start with four rounds of clubs. West follows on the first round and then discards two hearts and a spade. It is still not the moment to test the diamonds. Play your three spade winners instead. This will be the position as you lead the last spade winner from dummy:

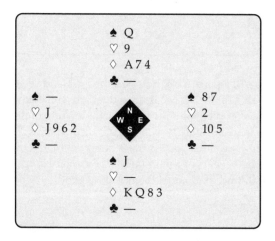

What can West throw on the last spade? If he throws the ♡J, dummy's ♡9 will be good trick. If he throws a diamond instead, you will score four diamond tricks. Slam made!

What happened on that last deal? West was squeezed – he was forced to throw away one of his red-suit guards. As you saw, it was not a particularly difficult hand to play. All you had to do was to leave until the last moment your play on the 4-3 suit. Did you have to watch carefully which cards were thrown? Not particularly. You needed to look out for the ♡J and the ♡10. If both of those were thrown, dummy's ♡9 would become good. If not, you would simply play the 4-3 diamond suit and hope to score four tricks from it.

It's not easy for East to see but if he refuses to win the first trick, allowing his partner's ♡Q to run to South's ♡K, the slam will go down. West can then discard three hearts, retaining the ♡J and his diamond guard.

On the final example you must delay your play in two 4-3 suits!

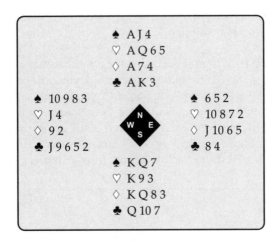

```
              ♠ A J 4
              ♡ A Q 6 5
              ◇ A 7 4
              ♣ A K 3
  ♠ 10 9 8 3              ♠ 6 5 2
  ♡ J 4         N         ♡ 10 8 7 2
  ◇ 9 2      W     E      ◇ J 10 6 5
  ♣ J 9 6 5 2    S        ♣ 8 4
              ♠ K Q 7
              ♡ K 9 3
              ◇ K Q 8 3
              ♣ Q 10 7
```

West leads the ♠10 against 7NT. You win the trick and see that you have twelve tricks on top. A 3-3 break in either red suit will give you the thirteenth trick you seek. Should you test these suits immediately? No! Win the spade lead and play two more rounds of spades. Then continue with three rounds of clubs. East is not a happy man. On the last club he must throw either a heart or a diamond. When you play the two red suits in turn, you will find that one of them is now good.

Tip

34

Attack against six of a suit, play safe against 6NT

W hat is the best general guideline for choosing an opening lead against a small slam? Should you make an attacking lead, hoping to score two quick tricks or perhaps set up a second trick for the defence? Or should you choose a safe lead, doing your best not to give away a trick? You should **attack against a six of a suit and play safe against 6NT**.

When players bid to a contract such as 6♡ they can usually make twelve tricks somehow or other if they are left in peace to establish them. Often they can set up a side suit to provide some discards. If you do not have a second trick ready to cash at the moment declarer surrenders the lead in the side suit, you are dead. Look at this typical deal:

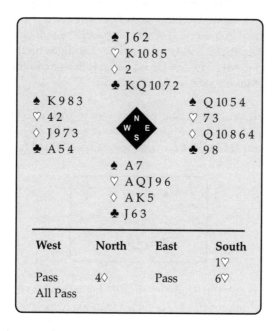

	♠ J 6 2		
	♡ K 10 8 5		
	◇ 2		
	♣ K Q 10 7 2		

♠ K 9 8 3		♠ Q 10 5 4
♡ 4 2	N	♡ 7 3
◇ J 9 7 3	W E	◇ Q 10 8 6 4
♣ A 5 4	S	♣ 9 8

	♠ A 7
	♡ A Q J 9 6
	◇ A K 5
	♣ J 6 3

West	North	East	South
			1♡
Pass	4◇	Pass	6♡
All Pass			

North's 4◇ is a splinter bid, showing a sound raise to game and at most one diamond. What opening lead would you choose, as West?

In the average club game you can be sure that at least half the West players will lead a trump. "I didn't want to give a trick away," they will say afterwards. You can see what will happen. Declarer will win the trump lead, draw trumps and knock out the ♣A. He can then throw his spade loser on dummy's established clubs, making twelve tricks easily.

Suppose next that the deal arose in a world championship. Almost every West player would attack by leading a spade! Why is that? They can see one defensive trick, the ♣A, and they want to set up a second trick before declarer can establish any discards. The lead succeeds here because East's ♠Q will remove South's ace in the suit. When declarer eventually plays on clubs, West will win with the ace and cash the ♠K to beat the slam.

You may be thinking: 'What if declarer held the ace and queen of spades?' It's entirely possible but bridge is a game of percentages. Experienced players keep in their memories not only the slam hands that they have defended themselves but all those they have read about. The general consensus is: **make an attacking lead against a small slam in a suit.**

Suppose next that you are on lead against 6NT. What should your general policy be then? Declarer does not now have the power of the trump suit to help him set up discards. Typically he will have something like ten or eleven tricks on top and will have to fight hard for the extra one or two tricks that he needs. Do not hand him an extra trick with your opening lead! **Make a safe lead against 6NT.**

From a given hand, many club players would make exactly the same lead against 6NT as they would have done against 3NT. Suppose the bidding has been 1NT – 3NT and you have to find a lead from this hand:

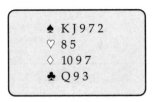

Not difficult, is it? You lead the 'fourth highest of your longest and strongest', reaching for the ♠7. Is such a lead likely to give away a trick? Yes, it might do. Declarer has the majority of the high cards and it is entirely possible that he will hold the ace and queen between his own hand and the dummy. You are willing to take the risk of giving away a trick, however, because to beat 3NT you need to set up five tricks for the defence. The spade suit gives you the best chance of doing this.

---

52 Great Bridge Tips

Next suppose that you hold the same hand and the bidding has been 1NT – 6NT. What would you lead now? Leading a spade would be a serious mistake. The opponents will surely hold at least 32 points, to bid a small slam in no-trumps, and it is now almost certain that the opponents hold both the ace and queen of spades. What's more, there is no point at all in taking such a risk. You don't need to set up five tricks now, so it is less attractive to lead a spade. Against 6NT you should look for a safe lead. Here you should lead the ◊10. Perhaps this is the full deal:

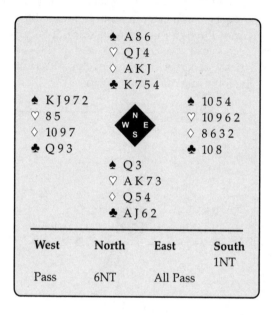

West	North	East	South
			1NT
Pass	6NT	All Pass	

Suppose you lead the ♠7, the 'fourth best of your longest and strongest'. With no option, declarer will play low in the dummy and win with the spade queen. After this lucky start, he will have eleven top tricks. He can establish an extra trick from the club suit and the slam will be his.

If you lead a safe ◊10, declarer will have only ten top tricks and will have to do his own work to seek two more. When he eventually takes the club finesse and this fails, the slam will go one down.

Note that a club lead would also surrender the slam. Leading away from an honour, against 6NT, is very dangerous. Look for a suit where you hold no honours. If you have more than one such suit, generally lead from the longest suit. If instead you lead from such as a small doubleton, you may pick up partner's Q-x-x or J-x-x-x.

Tip 35

Lead through a defender's ace

As I mentioned in a previous Tip, a defender regards an ace as a fishing net. He likes to catch a really big card in it, preferably a king or a queen. You can often put him to a difficult decision if you lead a low card through the defender's ace. If he plays the ace, he will catch only a couple of spot-cards. If instead he does not play the ace, you can steal a trick and perhaps start to develop tricks in a different suit. Deals such as the following are commonplace:

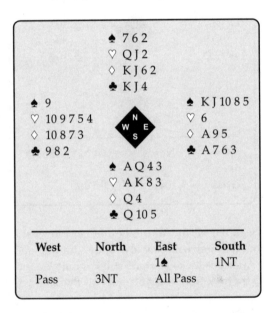

West	North	East	South
		1♠	1NT
Pass	3NT	All Pass	

West leads the ♣9 and East overtakes with the ♣10, which you win with the queen. How will you continue?

Suppose you lead the ◊Q next. East will win with the ace and clear the spade suit. With only eight tricks at your disposal (two spades, four hearts and two diamonds) you will go down. You can mark time by cashing the hearts but East has three easy club discards. The moment you play on clubs, East will pounce with the ace and cash his spades.

To make the contract you must cross to dummy with a heart at Trick 2 and lead a low diamond **through East's ace**, towards your hand. If East rises with the ◇A (catching only two minnow diamonds in his net), you will have three diamond tricks, enough for the contract. If instead he plays low, you will score a trick with the ◇Q. That will give you seven top tricks and you can set up two more by knocking out the ace of clubs.

In a suit contract such a play can gain in a different way: if the defender rises with the ace, he gives you an extra trick; if he does not, you will discard your remaining card in the suit. That's what happens here:

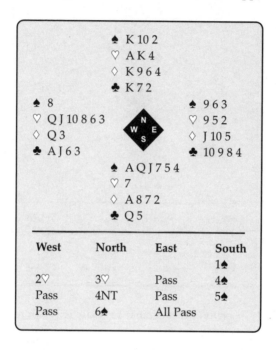

	♠ K 10 2	
	♡ A K 4	
	◇ K 9 6 4	
	♣ K 7 2	

West	North	East	South
			1♠
2♡	3♡	Pass	4♠
Pass	4NT	Pass	5♠
Pass	6♠	All Pass	

West leads the ♡Q and you win with the ace. How will you continue?

You should draw trumps in three rounds and lead the ♣5 **through West's ace,** towards the dummy. This leaves West with no winning option. If he rises with the ♣A, you will have two discards for your losing diamonds – one on the ♡K and another on the third round of clubs. If instead West plays low (not regarding the ♣5 as a big enough fish for his splendid net), dummy's king will win the trick. You can then throw the ♣Q on dummy's second heart winner. With no loser in the club suit you can set up the diamond suit. The 3-2 break means that you lose only one trick there and you make the small slam.

Suppose, on the last deal, that East had held the ♣A. The winning play would then be to lead a club from dummy, through East's ace and towards your queen. On this occasion West's overcall made it almost certain that he held the ♣A.

We have space for one more situation in which you can benefit by leading through a defender's ace. You sneak an extra trick and gain a further trick later, with an endplay.

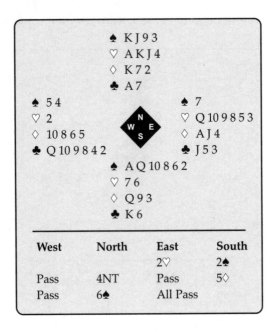

	♠ K J 9 3	
	♡ A K J 4	
	◊ K 7 2	
	♣ A 7	

	♠ K J 9 3		
♠ 5 4			♠ 7
♡ 2			♡ Q 10 9 8 5 3
◊ 10 8 6 5			◊ A J 4
♣ Q 10 9 8 4 2			♣ J 5 3
	♠ A Q 10 8 6 2		
	♡ 7 6		
	◊ Q 9 3		
	♣ K 6		

West	North	East	South
		2♡	2♠
Pass	4NT	Pass	5◊
Pass	6♠	All Pass	

West leads his singleton heart against 6♠. How will you play?

You win the heart lead with the ace and draw trumps in two rounds, ending in the dummy. You then lead a low diamond *through East's ace* towards the South hand. East has to duck or he will give you two diamond tricks and the contract. You win with the ◊Q and cash your remaining winners in the black suits, retaining ♡K-J and ◊K in the dummy. Which three cards can East keep? To prevent you from gaining an extra trick immediately, he has to keep ♡Q-9 and the ◊A. You then throw him in with a diamond to lead into dummy's ♡K-J.

Deals such as these arise very frequently. By leading through a defender's ace, you put him under pressure. On the deal we have just seen, there was nothing the defender could do. Sometimes he can beat the contract, provided he guesses what to do. Fortunately for the declarers of this world, defenders do not always guess right!

Tip 36

Do not misuse ace-asking bids

How do most people bid slams? There's not much doubt about the answer: very poorly! At some stage or other, one player reckons that he has values to spare for a game and there may be a slam available. Does he consult partner, to find out what his other half thinks? No, the preferred method is simply to ask for aces and then bid a slam provided two aces are not missing (or two key cards if you play Roman Key-Card Blackwood). When a minimum hand goes down in the dummy and the slam fails by a trick or two, the ace-asker will mutter: 'You didn't have very much for me.'

Most players misuse ace-asking bids. Instead of rushing for a Blackwood 4NT, or a Gerber 4♣, look for some way to consult your partner. Find out that he has 'not very much for you' before you bid a slam! The way to do that is to use control-showing cue-bids. In other words, when you have agreed a trump suit and want to suggest a slam, you bid a new suit (usually at the four-level or higher) to show the ace or king of that suit and to suggest a slam. On certain hands you can also make a cue-bid on a singleton or void, to show that you hold a control in the suit. Here is a typical start to an auction, involving a cue-bid:

West	East
1♡	1♠
3♠	4♢

Spades have been agreed as trumps, so East's 4♢ passes these messages:

(a) "I think a spade slam may be possible. What do you think?"
(b) "I have the ace or king of diamonds."
(c) "I do not have the ace or king of clubs."

Do you see what a powerful bid 4♢ is? It consults partner rather than simply saying "Tell me how many aces you have and I will make the decision!" On this occasion it will also allow the partnership to stop in game if there are two top club losers. What should West do next? He can cue-bid 4♡, if he holds a control (ace or king) in that suit, but only if he also has a club control. Obviously it is his duty to sign off if he knows that neither player has a club control and the opponents can cash the ace and king of clubs. Knowing that his partner is strong enough to consider a slam, West might also bid Blackwood.

Let's see some auctions where many (perhaps most) players would misuse ace-asking bids. We will assume that 4NT is Roman Key-Card Blackwood, where the four aces and the trump king count as key-cards.

```
   ♠ A Q J 9 6              ♠ K 10 4
   ♡ A K 10 5        N      ♡ 8 3
   ◊ 10 2         W     E   ◊ Q J 5
   ♣ K 9             S      ♣ A Q 10 6 3
```

Ace-asking Auction

1♠	2♣
2♡	4♠
4NT	5♡
6♠	

West has good trumps, extra values, and a precious king in partner's main suit. Very reasonably, he thinks that there may be a chance of a slam. Is it the right moment to bid 4NT? No! That's because he has two top losers in diamonds and 4NT will not tell him if East holds a diamond control. You can see how the ace-asking auction misfires. West arrives in 6♠ when the defenders have two tricks to cash in the unbid suit. This is how the hands should be bid:

Cue-bidding Auction

West	East
1♠	2♣
2♡	4♠
5♣	5♠

Spades have been agreed as trumps, so West's 5♣ is a control-showing cue-bid, telling partner that he has slam ambitions and the ace or king of clubs. Since East has no control to bid in either red suit, he signs off in 5♠ and the partnership stops in good time. West knows from his partner's failure to cue-bid 5◊ that the defenders have two top diamonds to cash.

On the next deal East is very strong and wants to be in a slam unless his partner's opening bid is a minimum one.

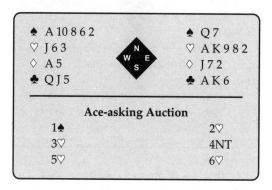

Ace-asking Auction	
1♠	2♡
3♡	4NT
5♡	6♡

East can see a chance of a slam, yes, but he is not strong enough to insist on one. With a hand such as East's you need to consult partner, to find out if he has any values to spare. This is how the bidding might go when East-West are playing cue-bids:

Cue-bidding Auction	
West	East
1♠	2♡
3♡	4♣
4◇	4♡

Although West has only a minimum opening, he is happy to show the ◇A when this does not take the bidding past game. That's because his partner is unlimited and might need to know about this card. East has already suggested a slam, so he bids just 4♡ at his next turn. He knows that his partner will bid again if he has anything to spare. With poor trumps and a completely minimum opening bid, West lets the bidding die.

We'll end with a pair of hands where many East players would incorrectly use Gerber:

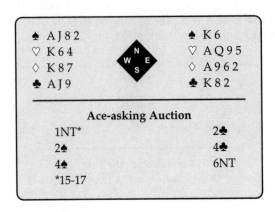

♠ A J 8 2		♠ K 6	
♡ K 6 4		♡ A Q 9 5	
◇ K 8 7		◇ A 9 6 2	
♣ A J 9		♣ K 8 2	

Ace-asking Auction

1NT*	2♣
2♠	4♣
4♠	6NT
*15-17	

Suppose you play that 4♣ is always Gerber in 1NT auctions, thereby precluding its use as a cue-bid. You bid 4♣ (Gerber) on those East cards and hear the best possible response: two aces. You advance to 6NT and, when dummy goes down, your partner will see that the contract is a very poor one.

What went wrong? Asking for aces was not the right action on the East hand. He needed to say instead: "Partner, please bid 6NT if your hand is maximum." This can be done by making a *limit bid of 4NT* on the second round:

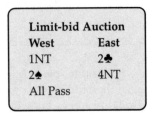

Limit-bid Auction

West	East
1NT	2♣
2♠	4NT
All Pass	

The opener would advance to 6NT on a maximum hand (perhaps containing only one ace) and pass 4NT on the present West hand (despite holding two aces). As you see, overall strength is the key factor when considering a no-trump slam on balanced hands. The number of aces held is less important. Indeed, since you need at least 33 points to even consider playing in 6NT with two balanced hands, there can never be two aces missing!

Tip 37

As declarer, play the highest of touching cards

Suppose you are the declarer in 3NT and West leads a suit where dummy holds 7-4 and you have K-Q-5. East plays the jack. Should you win with the queen or the king? Ask a group of players at your local club and at least one of them will reply: 'It doesn't make any difference, surely?' It can make a very real difference and you should generally win with the highest card from equals.

Let's look at a typical deal where you can put the defenders to a guess by following this Tip.

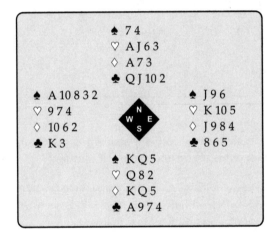

```
                    ♠ 7 4
                    ♡ A J 6 3
                    ◇ A 7 3
                    ♣ Q J 10 2
   ♠ A 10 8 3 2                    ♠ J 9 6
   ♡ 9 7 4            N             ♡ K 10 5
   ◇ 10 6 2      W        E         ◇ J 9 8 4
   ♣ K 3             S             ♣ 8 6 5
                    ♠ K Q 5
                    ♡ Q 8 2
                    ◇ K Q 5
                    ♣ A 9 7 4
```

West leads the ♠3 against your contract of 3NT and East plays the ♠J. How would you play the contract?

Let's see what is likely to happen if you ignore the Tip and win with the queen. You cross to the ◇A and run the ♣Q. The finesse loses to the king and West has to determine his next play. He knows that you hold the ♠K! Why is that? Because if East held the card he would have played it at Trick 1. When you won the first trick with the queen you gave West this valuable information. Since continuing spades will give you an extra trick in the suit (it would in fact give you the contract), West will surely switch to one of the red suits. The contract will now go down. With only eight top tricks available to you, there will be little option but to take the heart finesse. When it loses, East will lead a spade through your remaining honour and West will score four spade tricks.

Let's rewind the tape to the first trick and see what happens if you win the first trick with the king (the higher of your touching cards). Now life is not so easy for West. If East has played the ♠J at Trick 1 from a holding such as ♠Q-J-6, it may be essential for the defenders to cash four spade tricks at this moment. For example, the whole deal might be like this:

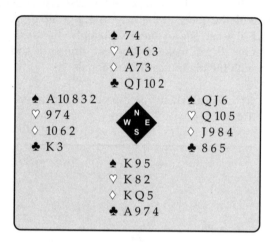

```
                    ♠ 7 4
                    ♡ A J 6 3
                    ◇ A 7 3
                    ♣ Q J 10 2
   ♠ A 10 8 3 2         N        ♠ Q J 6
   ♡ 9 7 4         W       E     ♡ Q 10 5
   ◇ 10 6 2            S        ◇ J 9 8 4
   ♣ K 3                         ♣ 8 6 5
                    ♠ K 9 5
                    ♡ K 8 2
                    ◇ K Q 5
                    ♣ A 9 7 4
```

If West fails to cash the four available spade tricks when the club finesse loses, you will win his return and claim the contract.

How can West know what to do in this situation? He can't! If you follow the Tip and win with the higher card, West will have to guess. Even the best players cannot guess right all the time.

This is a similar position:

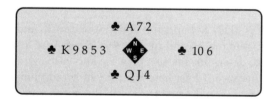

```
              ♣ A 7 2
   ♣ K 9 8 5 3     N        ♣ 10 6
              W       E
                  S
              ♣ Q J 4
```

West leads the ♣5 against 3NT. You play low from dummy and East plays the ♣10. If you win with the jack, West will know that you also hold the queen. Instead you should win with the queen. West will then have no idea where the ♣J is. When he regains the lead he may be tempted to continue the suit. You will then score three club tricks.

Note that this type of play is most likely to succeed when your cards are adjacent to East's card in value. Look at this spade suit:

West leads the ♠3 and East plays the ♠10. You will not fool West by winning with the king now, because he knows that if East held the ♠Q he would have played it. (It is still right to follow the Tip and win with the king, because this would leave West in doubt when he had led from ♠A-8-4-3-2, his partner holding ♠ J-10-5).

The Tip applies with equal force here:

There are almost certainly players at your local club who would lead a small card from dummy and finesse the ten, winning the trick. Do you see why this is wrong? You are giving away information to both the defenders. When the 10 wins, East knows that you hold A-Q-J-10. He therefore knows that you have seven points in the suit and four tricks. Such knowledge may greatly assist his defence. You should finesse the ◇Q instead. East will then have no idea where the ◇J and ◇10 are. Nor will he know that you have four tricks in the suit. This is a similar position:

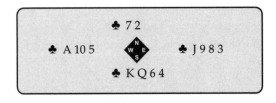

You lead a low card from dummy towards your honours. Suppose you play the ♣Q and West wins with the ace. East now knows that you hold the ♣K. Why is that? Firstly, because West might have led the suit if he held the ace and king. Secondly, because even if West did hold the ace and king of clubs he would have won the trick with the king.

It is standard in defence to play the lower of touching cards, precisely because you want to give information to your partner. As declarer, you don't want to give information to anyone. That is why you follow the opposite path and nearly always play the higher of touching cards.

Why did the words 'nearly always' creep into that last sentence? It's because you must sometimes turn a blind eye to the Tip when you hold ace-king in the suit that has been led. Look at this deal:

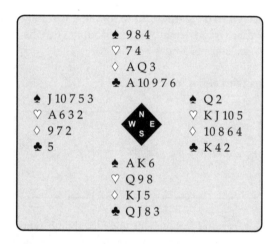

West leads the ♠5 against 3NT and East plays the ♠Q. Suppose you win with the ♠A (the higher of touching cards) and run the queen of clubs. Will a strong defender in the East seat return a spade now, giving you the contract? No. He will say to himself: "Why didn't declarer hold up the spade ace? He must have the king as well!" Taking his best chance, East will switch to the ♡J and your contract will be sunk.

Suppose you win the first trick with the ♠K instead. East cannot now exclude the possibility that his partner has led from ♠A-J-x-x-x. He is likely to return his partner's suit rather than risk hearing, "Why on earth did you switch to a heart, partner? We had four spade tricks to take!"

Tip 38

Remove the entry to dummy prematurely

One of the most common ways to play a suit contract is to draw trumps, set up a suit in dummy and then return to dummy to take discards on the established winners. As a defender, what can you do to prevent this? Sometimes you can remove the entry that declarer will need to the dummy. Take the West cards here and see if you can spot how to do this.

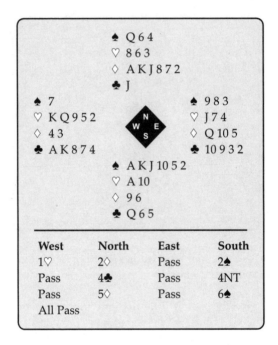

	♠ Q 6 4	
	♡ 8 6 3	
	◊ A K J 8 7 2	
	♣ J	
♠ 7		♠ 9 8 3
♡ K Q 9 5 2		♡ J 7 4
◊ 4 3		◊ Q 10 5
♣ A K 8 7 4		♣ 10 9 3 2
	♠ A K J 10 5 2	
	♡ A 10	
	◊ 9 6	
	♣ Q 6 5	

West	North	East	South
1♡	2◊	Pass	2♠
Pass	4♣	Pass	4NT
Pass	5◊	Pass	6♠
All Pass			

North's 4♣ was a splinter bid, showing a raise to 4♠ and at most one club. You lead the ♣A from the West hand. What will you do at Trick 2?

When this deal arose, West switched to the ♡K. Declarer won with the ace and drew two rounds of trumps with the ace and king. The time had come to set up the diamonds. Declarer cashed the ace and king of diamonds and ruffed a diamond. He then crossed to the ♠Q and discarded one heart and two clubs on the three established diamonds.

How could the contract have been beaten? It should be clear to West that the slam will be cold unless East has a diamond guard. It follows that declarer will have to ruff the diamonds good and then reach dummy by 'drawing trumps, ending in the dummy'. If East has three trumps, West can spoil declarer's plan by forcing dummy to ruff at Trick 2.

What can declarer do if West continues with the ♣K at Trick 2? His best chance is to ruff, draw trumps and then rely on the diamond finesse. The ◇J loses to East's ◇Q and the slam is one down. Once West kills the trump entry to dummy, declarer cannot recover.

When defending at notrumps, removing an entry to dummy can be a higher priority than setting up your long suit. Take the East cards here.

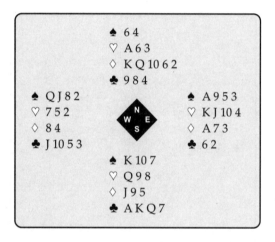

After a 1NT – 3NT auction, West leads a fourth-best ♠2 and you win with the ace. What will you do next?

Suppose you give the matter little thought and return the ♠3. Declarer knows from the lead of the ♠2 that spades are breaking 4-4. He will rise with the king and clear the diamond suit. Nothing can then prevent him from scoring four diamonds, three clubs and one trick in each major suit.

What should your thoughts be, when you are considering your return at Trick 2? You should reason that declarer is most unlikely to make the contract unless he can take full advantage of the diamond suit. To prevent declarer scoring four diamond tricks, it is necessary to knock out the ♡A. So, at Trick 2 you must make a spectacular switch to the ♡K! Declarer cannot afford to duck this because a switch back to spades will then give the defenders three spades, one heart and one diamond.

Declarer wins with the ♡A, therefore and plays on diamonds. West shows his doubleton by playing the ◇8 on the first round, followed by the ◇4. Since this leaves declarer with three diamonds, you hold up the ◇A until the third round and then clear the spades. Declarer has eight tricks on top now: one spade, two hearts, two diamonds and three clubs. His only realistic hope of a ninth trick is that the clubs will break 3-3. Not today and the excellent defence beats the game by one trick.

For our final example, let's go back to a suit contract. Take the West cards here and see if you can visualize how declarer will play the contract. See also if you can think of a way to spoil his plans.

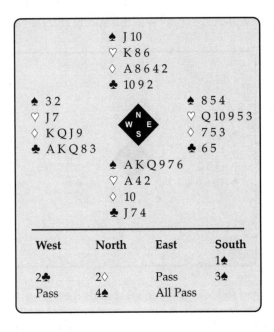

```
                 ♠ J 10
                 ♡ K 8 6
                 ◇ A 8 6 4 2
                 ♣ 10 9 2
    ♠ 3 2                        ♠ 8 5 4
    ♡ J 7           N            ♡ Q 10 9 5 3
    ◇ K Q J 9    W     E         ◇ 7 5 3
    ♣ A K Q 8 3     S            ♣ 6 5
                 ♠ A K Q 9 7 6
                 ♡ A 4 2
                 ◇ 10
                 ♣ J 7 4
```

West	North	East	South
			1♠
2♣	2◇	Pass	3♠
Pass	4♠	All Pass	

You cash three clubs successfully against South's 4♠. What next?

At the table West switched to the ◇K. Declarer won with the ace and ruffed a diamond. A trump to the jack was followed by a second diamond ruff and a trump to the 10, both defenders following. A third diamond ruff set up a long card in the suit and declarer drew the last trump. The ♡K remained as an entry to dummy, so declarer was able to reach the long diamond and discard his losing heart. Game made!

How could West prevent this? It was not possible to dislodge the ♡K but West could have removed one of dummy's entries by switching to a trump. Unable to enjoy a long diamond, declarer would be one down

When you are guaranteed all the tricks in a suit, it may seem irrelevant how you play it. Think again! Sometimes you can create extra entries to the weaker hand by overtaking one high card with another.

Let's see some full-deal examples of this sort of entry-creating play.

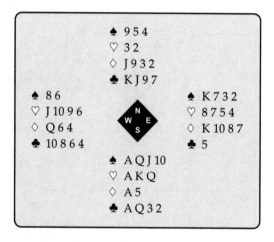

How would you tackle 6NT when West leads the ♡J?

Four spade tricks will give you the slam and you would like to be able to take the spade finesse three times, in case East holds ♠K-x-x-x. How should you play the clubs to provide the necessary entries? After winning the heart lead, you should cash the ace of clubs. You then lead the queen of clubs. When West follows to this trick it is safe to overtake with dummy's ♣K. East shows out but this causes no problem. You play a spade to the queen, breathing more freely when the finesse wins. You can then reach dummy for a second time by finessing the ♣9. After repeating the spade finesse you play a club to the jack, entering dummy for the third time. You finesse in spades once again and land the slam.

What would have happened if West had shown out on the second round of clubs, when you led the queen? You could not then have afforded to overtake the ♣Q. You would have played low from dummy and entered dummy just twice, on the third and fourth round of clubs. You would have had to hope that East's ♣K was not guarded three times and that two finesses would suffice.

The same style of play may be necessary even when you will have to concede a trick in the suit involved.

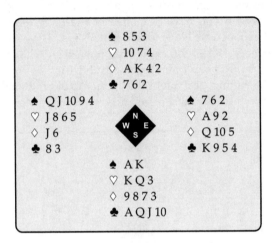

West leads the ♠Q against 3NT. How will you play the contract?

The best plan is to aim for four club tricks, three diamond tricks and two spades. You will need to find East with the ♣K. If he holds four cards in the club suit you will need to take the club finesse three times. How can you create three entries to the dummy for this purpose? By some clever work in the diamond suit!

You win the spade lead with the ace and lead the ◊9 to dummy's ace. You take a successful club finesse and then lead the ◊8 to dummy's king. A second club finesse wins and West follows suit. The time has come to set up a diamond trick. Do you lead the ◊3 from your hand? No, because you will need this card to reach dummy on the fourth round of diamonds. You lead the ◊7 to East's queen. East is welcome to set up the spade suit. When you win the second round of spades, you will lead your ◊3 and (trying hard not to look pleased with yourself) overtake with dummy's ◊4. You can then finesse in clubs for a third time, picking up four tricks from the suit and making the contract. Since East did hold ♣K-x-x-x, and three club finesses were needed, this was the only way to make the contract.

Tip

40

**With points to spare,
bid 6NT rather
than six of a suit**

How do you choose between bidding 6NT and a small slam in a suit? When you have 34 points or more and both hands are balanced, you are likely to find that 6NT is best, even if you have a 4-4 fit elsewhere. When you are attempting a slam with around 31-32 points, it may be that you cannot make twelve tricks without adding a trick or two by ruffing. You might then prefer to bid the small slam in a 4-4 fit. Here is typical deal where you need to bid 6♡ instead of 6NT:

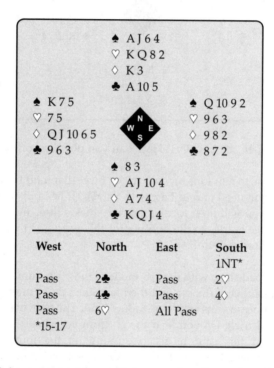

	♠ A J 6 4		
	♡ K Q 8 2		
	◊ K 3		
	♣ A 10 5		

♠ K 7 5	♠ Q 10 9 2
♡ 7 5	♡ 9 6 3
◊ Q J 10 6 5	◊ 9 8 2
♣ 9 6 3	♣ 8 7 2

	♠ 8 3		
	♡ A J 10 4		
	◊ A 7 4		
	♣ K Q J 4		

West	North	East	South
			1NT*
Pass	2♣	Pass	2♡
Pass	4♣	Pass	4◊
Pass	6♡	All Pass	
*15-17			

Once North hears of a 4-4 heart fit, he can visualize a slam. He jumps to 4♣. Is this Gerber? Many players would treat it as such but it is not the best way to play the bid (see Tip 36). It is better to use such jumps to the four-level as control-showing cue-bids. In this way you invite partner's cooperation rather than saying to him 'Tell me how many aces you have and I will make the decision.' Here South is happy to cooperate with a cue-bid in diamonds. North has heard enough and leaps to 6♡.

It's a good contract, as you see. Only 32 points but the trump suit is compact, with all the top cards. You can count 11 top tricks and a diamond ruff in dummy will give you a twelfth. Prospects in 6NT would be poor, not much better than finding West with the ♠K-Q.

Now let's look at a typical deal when you have upwards of 34 points. With two balanced hands facing each other, you will then have a good chance of making twelve tricks in notrumps. It will be an unnecessary risk to play in a 4-4 fit, where a bad trump break may cost you the slam.

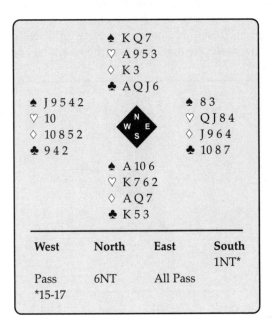

West	North	East	South
			1NT*
Pass	6NT	All Pass	
*15-17			

How should North bid his hand when he hears a strong 1NT from partner? As on the previous deal, he has a possible ruffing value in diamonds but there are two reasons why he might shy away from a 4-4 heart fit. Firstly, he holds 19 points, so a slam might be cold in notrumps on sheer power while a bad trump break may defeat the suit slam. Secondly, his own hearts are not so brilliant. A-9-5-3 opposite some random four-card holding might easily produce two trump losers, even when twelve tricks are cold in notrumps.

In the diagram there are indeed twelve top tricks in 6NT. Playing in 6♡, you have quite good chances. You are safe when hearts break 3-2. You are safe also when you cash the ♡K and a singleton queen, jack or ten appears from East. (You can then lead towards the A-9, planning to insert the 9 if West does not split his honours.) When East holds four trumps, or a singleton that is not an honour, you will go down.

Two deals prove nothing in themselves and if you are the sceptical sort you may think that the hands were specially chosen to support the Tip. (As if a highly respected bridge writer would dream of doing such a thing!) The deals are by way of illustration only. Bridge players know from experience that two balanced hands containing 34 points upwards will usually generate good play for 6NT. They also have unpleasant memories of going down in suit slams when a carefully located 4-4 fit turned sour and there were two unavoidable losers in the trump suit.

Another reason to prefer 6NT, when you have sufficient points, is that you may avoid an adverse ruff. That was the case when this deal arose:

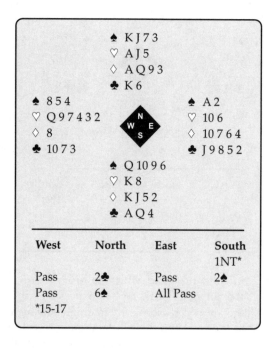

	♠ K J 7 3		
	♡ A J 5		
	◊ A Q 9 3		
	♣ K 6		

♠ 8 5 4		♠ A 2
♡ Q 9 7 4 3 2		♡ 10 6
◊ 8		◊ 10 7 6 4
♣ 10 7 3		♣ J 9 8 5 2

	♠ Q 10 9 6		
	♡ K 8		
	◊ K J 5 2		
	♣ A Q 4		

West	North	East	South
			1NT*
Pass	2♣	Pass	2♠
Pass	6♠	All Pass	
*15-17			

North decided to bid the small slam in the 4-4 spade fit, rather than in notrumps. West led his singleton ◊8 and the slam was doomed. When declarer played on trumps, East won and gave partner a diamond ruff.

Declarer was unlucky that diamonds were 4-1, yes. He was also unlucky that the defender with the singleton diamond was on lead and that the trump ace lay in the opposite hand. The fact remains that 6NT was a safer contract. After knocking out the ace of spades declarer would have twelve easy tricks, not even needing the heart finesse.

S ometimes declarer misses a chance to make a contract because he does not visualize the problem that a certain play may cause a defender. Put the defenders under pressure and a bundle of extra contracts will fall your way. Would you have spotted a chance to make this contract?

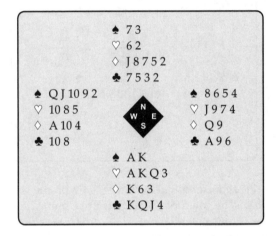

West leads the ♠Q against 3NT. How would you play the contract?

It doesn't look too promising, does it? You have only five tricks on top and the clubs will provide only three more, even if the suit breaks 3-2. As soon as the defenders gain the lead they will clear the spade suit and you will have no way to seek a ninth trick. Even so, the contract was made at the table. Can you guess how?

Declarer won the spade lead with the king and immediately led the king of diamonds. West placed declarer with something like K-Q-x in the suit and held up the ◇A, aiming to cut declarer off from the dummy. With the air of a man reprieved from the gallows, declarer switched his attention to the club suit. He was rewarded by a 3-2 break there and soon had nine tricks before him.

How did declarer spot this deceptive play? He realized that whenever the ace and queen of diamonds were in different hands the defender holding the ace would be faced with a big problem. Was it a mistake for West to hold up the ◊A? As the cards lay, yes, but he had no way of telling this. Had declarer held a more likely K-Q-x in the diamond suit it might have been a costly mistake for West not to hold up the ace.

Here is another deal where there is a chance to pose one of the defenders a problem. Would you have seen it?

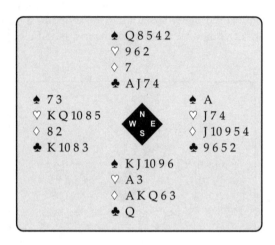

West led the ♡K against 6♠ and declarer won with the ace. With a loser exposed in hearts, he could not play on trumps immediately. He would have to dispose of his potential heart loser first. One chance was to play the three top diamonds, throwing two heart losers from dummy. The other was to run the ♣Q, aiming to throw the heart loser from the South hand. Which is the better chance, would you say?

The original declarer rated the club finesse as a 50% chance. Since a 4-3 diamond break was a 62% chance, this was the option he chose. His luck was out when West ruffed the third diamond. Declarer could overruff in dummy but, since there was no entry to the South hand, he could not switch horses and attempt the club finesse. 'Typical of my luck,' he informed his partner. 'The club finesse was right all the time!'

What did you make of that? Suppose declarer leads the ♣Q at Trick 2. Is there not a good chance that West will cover when he holds the ♣K? If West does cover, you can win with the ♣A and discard your heart loser on the ♣J. If no cover comes, you have lost nothing! You can play the three top diamonds anyway, reverting to the original declarer's line. By foreseeing the problem that West will face when you proffer the ♣Q at an early stage, you greatly increase your chance of making the slam.

The next deal is similar. Again you have a choice of lines to follow.

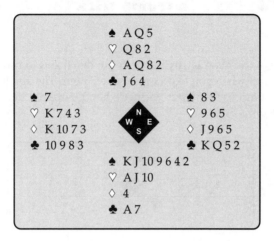

West leads the ♣10 against your contract of 6♠ and you win with the ace. How will you play the slam?

If West holds the ♡K, you have an unavoidable loser in that suit and must take the diamond finesse in a desperate attempt to avoid a club loser. If the ♡K is onside, though, you can afford a club loser. A diamond finesse would put the contract at risk in that case. If it failed, you would lose a diamond and a club. So, what is it to be?

As on the last deal, you can present a defender with a big problem by leading a queen. After drawing trumps, you should lead the ♡Q from dummy. It will be an awkward moment for East if he holds the ♡K. He is likely to shrug his shoulders and cover with the king. Now you know that you do not need to risk a diamond finesse. When the cards lie as in the diagram, East will not cover the ♡Q. It is then reasonable to assume that West has the king of hearts. You rise with the heart ace and take the diamond finesse. Success! The finesse wins and you can throw your club loser on the ◇A.

Tip 42

Ruff high to promote a trump trick

O
ne of the most satisfying moves in defence is to ruff with a high trump when you expect to be overruffed. The aim is to promote a trump trick in your partner's hand. Suppose declarer is in 4♠ with this trump suit:

It's his lucky day, isn't it? When he plays the ace and king, the suit will break 2-2 and he won't lose a trump trick. That's all true if has an early chance to draw trumps. Suppose instead that West can lead a suit that both East and South can ruff. If East ruffs with the queen, this will force the ace or king from declarer. West's ♠J will then score a trick.

The technique is known as an 'uppercut'. East delivers a solid blow with the queen of trumps, knocking out South's king. Let's see the play in the context of a full deal.

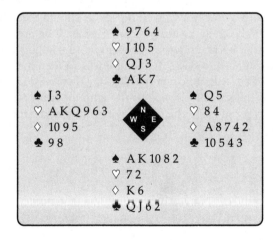

West, who overcalled 2♡, leads the ♡K against South's spade game. Take the East cards and see if you can find the right defence.

West cashes the ♡A at Trick 2 and continues with the ♡6, covered with dummy's jack. How do you defend? If you ruff with the ♠5, declarer will overruff and draw trumps, making his game easily. Instead you must ruff with the queen. Declarer overruffs and now has to lose a trump trick to West's jack. He has a diamond loser too and will go one down.

Why did West, your partner, lead a low heart on the third round instead of the ♡Q? Because he wanted to make it obvious to you that you should ruff. Some defenders in the East seat would have thought: 'South must hold the ♡Q, so I can afford to ruff with the five'. Do you see why that is wrong? Firstly, if declarer does have another heart you can see that you will beat the contract by ruffing with the queen and cashing the ♢A. Secondly, even if you do not hold the ♢A it cannot possibly cost to ruff with the queen instead of the 5. The ♠Q is useless, sitting under declarer's trumps, unless you attempt an uppercut with it.

It is your partner's duty to tell you when to ruff. Look at this deal:

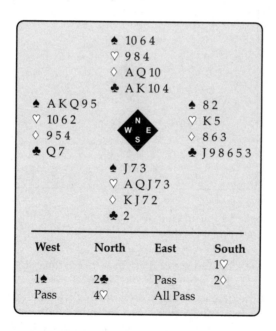

West	North	East	South
			1♡
1♠	2♣	Pass	2♢
Pass	4♡	All Pass	

West leads the ♠K and you signal with the ♠8. On the next round your partner plays the ♠A and declarer follows with the ♠J. What is your reaction when partner leads the ♠Q at Trick 3?

Since declarer followed with the ♠J on the previous trick, you may think that he has no spades left and that you should ruff this third round of spades with the ♡K, attempting an uppercut. Declarer would then be a happy man. He would follow suit on the third round of spades and then draw trumps and claim the contract when he regained the lead. To beat the contract, you must allow partner's ♠Q to win the third round of the suit and then ruff a fourth round of spades (yes, it gives a ruff-and-discard, but that is the only way to beat the contract) with the ♡K. Declarer overruffs with the ♡A and your partner's ♡10 is promoted.

How could you tell which round of spades to ruff? It was your partner's duty to tell you by leading a low spade on the round that you needed to ruff. If declarer had only two spades, West would have led a low spade on the third round, inviting you to ruff with your highest trump.

We'll end with a spectacular example of an uppercut, one that again involves giving declarer a ruff-and-discard.

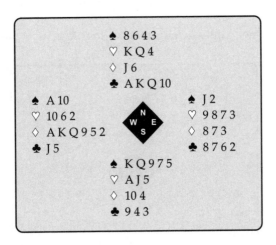

West, who opened 1◊, leads the ◊K against South's spade game. Do you see how the contract can be beaten?

West cashes the king and ace of diamonds, his partner signalling an odd number of cards by playing the ◊3 followed by the ◊7. It is barely possible that the defenders can score a further trick in the side suits, so West aims for two trump tricks. He continues with a third round of diamonds, giving declarer a (useless) ruff-and-discard. When declarer plays a trump to the king, West wins with the ace and leads a fourth round of diamonds. Now comes the uppercut. East ruffs with the ♠J, forcing South's ♠Q and West's ♠10 is promoted into the setting trick.

---

52 Great Bridge Tips

Tip 43

Many a trump promotion by the defenders could have been avoided if declarer had only seen it coming in time. One way to prevent a trump promotion is to break the communications between the two defenders. That's what you must do on this deal:

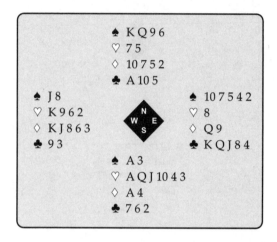

```
              ♠ K Q 9 6
              ♡ 7 5
              ◇ 10 7 5 2
              ♣ A 10 5
♠ J 8                        ♠ 10 7 5 4 2
♡ K 9 6 2          N         ♡ 8
◇ K J 8 6 3    W       E     ◇ Q 9
♣ 9 3              S         ♣ K Q J 8 4
              ♠ A 3
              ♡ A Q J 10 4 3
              ◇ A 4
              ♣ 7 6 2
```

West leads the ♣9 against your heart game. How would you play the contract?

Let's see first what happened when the deal was originally played. Declarer won the opening lead with dummy's ♣A and took a losing trump finesse. West led his remaining club and East scored two tricks in the suit. East now tried his luck with a fourth round of clubs and this promoted West's ♡9. One down!

How could declarer have avoided this trump promotion? He should have ducked the opening lead, allowing East to win the first round of clubs. Since many players lead the second best from a holding of small cards (see Tip 6), the lead of a 9 is usually either a singleton or top of a doubleton. If West held two clubs, holding up the ♣A for one round would break communications between the two defenders. It would prevent West from crossing to the East hand for a trump promotion. If instead the lead was a singleton, ducking could not cost. If West ruffed the club return, he would be ruffing a loser.

A different way to break the defenders' communications is the famous Scissors Coup. By throwing a singleton away, a loser-on-loser play, you prevent the defenders from crossing in that suit for a trump promotion (or a ruff). Here is a typical example of the technique:

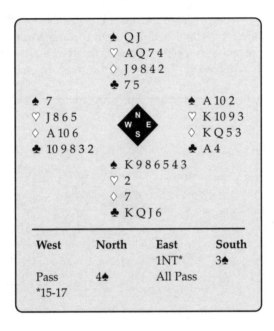

	♠ Q J	
	♡ A Q 7 4	
	◇ J 9 8 4 2	
	♣ 7 5	

♠ 7   ♠ A 10 2
♡ J 8 6 5   ♡ K 10 9 3
◇ A 10 6   ◇ K Q 5 3
♣ 10 9 8 3 2 ♣ A 4

	♠ K 9 8 6 5 4 3	
	♡ 2	
	◇ 7	
	♣ K Q J 6	

West	North	East	South
		1NT*	3♠
Pass	4♠	All Pass	
*15-17			

West leads the ♣10 against your game in spades. East wins with the ♣A and returns the ♣4 to your king. How would you tackle the play?

You can see what will happen if you simply play a trump to the queen now. East will win with the ♠A and cross to his partner's hand with a diamond. West can tell that his partner has no more clubs because he would not have returned the ♣4 from A-Q-J-4, A-Q-4 or A-J-4. He will therefore switch back to clubs, with fatal effect. If you ruff with the ♠J, East's ♠10 will be promoted. If instead you discard from dummy, East will score a ruff. One down either way.

How can you avoid this fate? You need to prevent East from crossing to his partner's hand in diamonds. Instead of leading a trump at Trick 3, you should play a heart to the ace. You then continue with the ♡Q. When East covers with the king, you discard your singleton diamond. This loser-on-loser play does not gain a trick directly. It does, however, prevent East from reaching his partner's hand at any stage. You will win

East's return and play a trump to the queen and ace. The defenders are powerless and you will be able to draw trumps when you regain the lead.

We will end with another deal where the original declarer suffered a trump promotion. Watch as the play is described and see if you could have avoided the same fate.

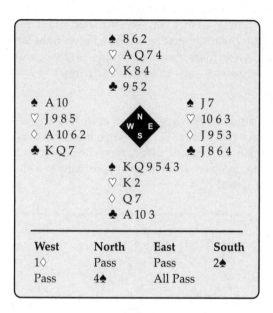

West	North	East	South
1◇	Pass	Pass	2♠
Pass	4♠	All Pass	

West led the ♣K against the spade game and declarer won the first trick. Since four losers were staring him the face, his next move was to play three top hearts, throwing one of his club losers. With that important business out of the way, he played a trump to the king and ace.

West cashed the ♣Q, declarer following with the 10. He continued with the ◇A, giving the defenders three tricks. Seeking a vital fourth trick, West next led the ♡J. East knew what to do. He ruffed with the ♠J and this promoted a trump trick for West's ♠10. That was one down.

How could the trump promotion have been avoided? There was no question of breaking communications on this deal, because West did all the damage and he held plenty of entries. The solution was for declarer to play the fourth round of hearts himself, discarding his last club. This would not gain a trick directly because he would be throwing one loser on another. It would, however, prevent West from leading the fourth heart himself later. No trump promotion would be possible.

Tip

44

**Seek a signal
to guide your
defence**

Why do you and your partner signal to each other when you are defending? So that you can exchange information and have a better chance of getting a key decision right later in the play. No great words of wisdom there. What is not so obvious is that you must sometimes take special steps to allow your partner to assist you with a signal.

One common situation is when declarer is in 3NT and is attempting to knock out an ace that you hold. Even when it will make no difference to declarer's communications, it may pay you to hold up the ace for an extra round. By doing so, you will give your partner a chance to signal. Here is a typical deal:

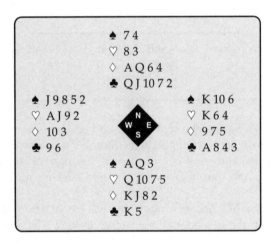

You are East and your partner leads the ♠5 against 3NT. Declarer wins your king with the ace and plays the ♣K, which you allow to hold. When he plays a second round of clubs, your partner follows and the queen is played from dummy. How will you conduct the defence?

Suppose you win the second round of clubs. Will you play the ♠10 next, returning partner's suit, or will you switch to hearts, hoping for four tricks there? The answer is that you would have to guess. On the evidence available so far, it would no doubt be better to continue

---

partner's suit, hoping that he had led from something like ♣Q-10-8-5-2. Declarer might then have won the first spade to retain his ♠J-x as a partial stopper if West held the club ace.

There is no need to put yourself to such a guess. If you win the third round of clubs rather than the second, partner will have the chance to make an informative discard. Here he will throw a spade. Since he would not throw a winner away, the message of a spade discard (whatever discarding method you happen to play) is that he does not want a spade return. Your partner knows, from your play of the ♠K, that declarer holds the ♠Q and that a spade return will probably allow him to run nine tricks. You switch to a low heart, therefore, and declarer cannot avoid the loss of four tricks in the suit. If your partner did hold Q-10-8-5-2 in the spade suit and wanted a spade return, he would have discarded a heart instead.

When you are defending a suit contract, it often happens that declarer has some quick discards available and you need to cash your available winners immediately. How can you know what to do? East found the right answer on this deal. Would you have done?

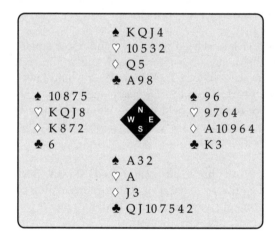

South arrives in 5♣, after an auction that need not concern us, and West (your partner) leads the ♡K. Declarer wins with the ♡A and runs the ♣Q to your king. How would you have continued the defence with those East cards?

An immediate heart return is not a good idea, for two reasons. Declarer might ruff the second heart when you had two diamonds to cash. Even if West can take one more heart trick, he may then do the wrong thing at

Trick 4, perhaps trying to cash another heart.

Instead of returning a heart, you should play the $\diamond$A. Partner's signal will now tell you what to do. (See Tip 10: an ace lead asks for an attitude signal, a king lead asks for a count signal.) If partner does not hold the $\diamond$K he will discourage diamonds, playing his lowest card in the suit. If he does hold the $\diamond$K, he must tell you whether to play a heart or a diamond. If declarer has only one more red card and this is a diamond, West will encourage a diamond continuation. If declarer's last red card is a heart, West will discourage a diamond continuation even if he holds the $\diamond$K.

You have a question on your lips, I realize. 'How on earth can West know how many cards declarer holds in each of the red suits?' Good question! The answer is that he has no idea whether declarer holds another diamond, but he has a good idea about the heart situation because (see Tip 10) you will have given a count signal at Trick 1, when the king of hearts was led. On the present layout, you will have signalled with the $\heartsuit$7 at Trick 1 (second highest from four small). This marks you with an even number of hearts and declarer with an odd number, doubtless just one here. Not expecting a second round of hearts to stand up, West will encourage a diamond continuation, dropping the $\diamond$8. A second diamond from you will then sink the contract.

Suppose declarer had started with $\heartsuit$A-6 and a low singleton diamond. How would the defence have gone then? You would signal with your lowest heart (from $\heartsuit$9-7-4) at Trick 1 and West would know that declarer held a second heart. When the $\diamond$A was played, West would discourage diamonds, even though he held the $\diamond$K. He would then win your heart return. With the contract already defeated, he could try his luck with the $\diamond$K, looking for two down.

Did you find all of that a bit complicated? It was. Such an effort is worthwhile if you want to succeed at this game. With a combination of count signals (on king leads) and attitude signals on ace (or queen) leads, you can solve most cash-out dilemmas.

Here is one more deal where, as East, you can seek assistance from your partner.

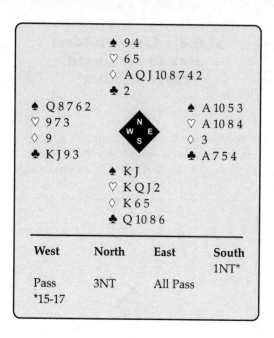

	♠ 9 4		
	♡ 6 5		
	◇ A Q J 10 8 7 4 2		
	♣ 2		

♠ Q 8 7 6 2		♠ A 10 5 3
♡ 9 7 3		♡ A 10 8 4
◇ 9		◇ 3
♣ K J 9 3		♣ A 7 5 4

	♠ K J		
	♡ K Q J 2		
	◇ K 6 5		
	♣ Q 10 8 6		

West	North	East	South
			1NT*
Pass	3NT	All Pass	
*15-17			

West leads the ♣6 against 3NT and you win with the ace, South following with the jack. What do you do next?

It is fairly obvious that if declarer gains the lead he will gallop past the finishing post. The fall of his ♣J at Trick 1 suggests that he may hold ♣K-J or ♣Q-J doubleton. Another possibility (See Tip 9 on false-carding at Trick 1) is that declarer holds ♣K-J-2 and has played the ♣J to encourage a spade continuation. How can you find out what to do next?

The answer is that you should cash the two aces in the other side suits, seeking an attitude signal from partner. When you play the ♡A, partner signals discouragement with the ♡3. When you continue with the ♣A the news is better, West signals encouragement with the ♣9. You play another club and – to sighs of relief from both defenders – the contract goes one down.

You would also have beaten the contract if West held ♠K-8-7-6-2 and neither the heart king nor the club king. He would then give a discouraging signal on both your aces and you would switch back to spades.

Tip 45

Make a loser-on-loser play to set up an extra winner

Sometimes you have no loser in a suit but, by conceding a trick there, you can establish an extra winner. It's the type of play that is often missed, so let's see a full-deal example straight away.

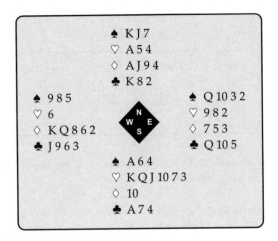

```
              ♠ K J 7
              ♡ A 5 4
              ◇ A J 9 4
              ♣ K 8 2
  ♠ 9 8 5              ♠ Q 10 3 2
  ♡ 6          N       ♡ 9 8 2
  ◇ K Q 8 6 2  W   E   ◇ 7 5 3
  ♣ J 9 6 3        S   ♣ Q 10 5
              ♠ A 6 4
              ♡ K Q J 10 7 3
              ◇ 10
              ♣ A 7 4
```

West leads the ◇K against your small slam in hearts. How will you play?

If you count the losers in the South hand, you will see that you have one loser in clubs and one possible loser in spades. How can you reduce the loser count to just one? Finessing the ♠J is one possibility. Half the time you will be lucky, half the time the finesse will lose and you will have put a cold slam on the floor!

How can you make certain of twelve tricks? You win the ◇K lead with the ace, draw trumps and lead the ◇J, throwing one of your potential losers from your hand. West wins the trick with the ◇Q but dummy's ◇9 is established. You will therefore be able to discard your second loser. In effect you swapped your two black-suit losers for one diamond loser. Good business! Note that you needed to make a plan before playing to Trick 1 (always a good idea). Otherwise you might forget that your diamond singleton had been the 10 and that the J-9 were equals against West's queen.

---

52 Great Bridge Tips

Let's see another example of this technique.

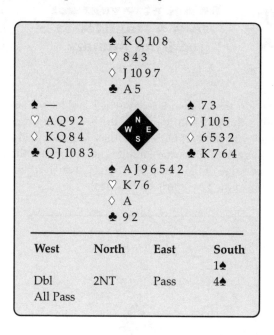

♠ K Q 10 8
♡ 8 4 3
◊ J 10 9 7
♣ A 5

♠ —
♡ A Q 9 2
◊ K Q 8 4
♣ Q J 10 8 3

♠ 7 3
♡ J 10 5
◊ 6 5 3 2
♣ K 7 6 4

♠ A J 9 6 5 4 2
♡ K 7 6
◊ A
♣ 9 2

West	North	East	South
			1♠
Dbl	2NT	Pass	4♠
All Pass			

North's 2NT showed a sound limit raise in spades. How would you play 4♠ when West leads the ♣Q?

You win the first trick and play a trump to the ace. After unblocking the ◊A, you return to dummy with a trump and run the ◊J, throwing your club loser. West wins with the ◊Q but he cannot play on hearts without conceding a trick to your king. He will probably exit with a second round of clubs, which you ruff. You cross to dummy with a third round of trumps and lead the ◊10, throwing a heart loser. West wins with the diamond king and still cannot safely play a heart. Since your ◊9 is now established, the game is yours. You will lose just two diamonds and a heart.

Look back at what happened. You started the deal with three heart losers and one club loser. By making two loser-on-loser plays, you swapped a club and a heart loser for two diamond losers – a fair trade. The benefit came when you set up an extra winner in the process.

Tip 46

Do not play your ace when a singleton is led from dummy

What do most defenders do when a side-suit singleton is led from dummy and they hold the ace in second position? They rise with the ace! Otherwise they fear they will never make a trick with it. It's a natural reaction but it is nearly always the wrong thing to do. Let's see some of the many situations in which it can give declarer the contract. Take the East cards on this deal:

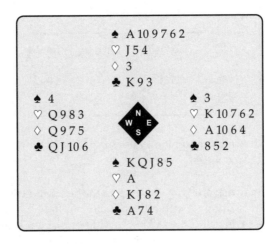

Your partner leads the ♣Q against a small slam in spades and declarer wins in hand with the ace. He crosses to the ace of trumps, your partner following, and leads the ◊3 from dummy. How would you defend?

Having read the title of this chapter a few moments ago, it is easy enough to play low from the East hand! The question is: would you have played low at the table? Let's see first what will happen if you do what most defenders would do and rise with the ace. Declarer will win your return and throw a club from dummy on his ◊K. He can then ruff a club in dummy and make the slam.

How will declarer play if you duck smoothly when the singleton diamond is led? Since most defenders leap in with the ace when they hold it, he will surely place the ace with West. In that case he will play the ◊J from his hand, hoping that you hold the queen and that the jack

will force West's ace. The contract will then go down. The ◊J will lose to
the queen and West will return another club. Declarer will no doubt take
two diamond ruffs, hoping to bring down the ace, but your ◊A will
survive this assault. Eventually declarer will have to lose a club and that
will be one down. That's one good reason to duck when you hold the ace,
then. You may give declarer a guess in the suit.

Another reason to play low is that rising with the ace may set up a
ruffing finesse against your partner. That's what would happen here:

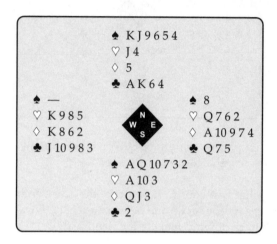

South arrived in six spades. A heart lead would have worked well, as it
happens, but West leads the ♣J. View the proceedings from the East seat
now. Declarer rises with dummy's ♣A and leads the singleton ◊5. How
should you react?

Once again you should play low. For one thing, declarer's diamonds
may be headed by the K-J as on the previous deal. If you rise with the
ace, or even pause to think about it, you will save him a guess. Here
South's diamonds are weaker, but it will still cost the contract if you play
your ace on dummy's singleton. Declarer will win your return, draw
your lone trump and lead the ◊Q, taking a ruffing finesse against West's
king. Whether or not West covers with the ◊Q with the ◊K, declarer will
eventually enjoy a discard of dummy's heart loser.

That's a second reason to play low, then. If you play high you may set up
a ruffing finesse against your partner.

A final reason to play low is that you may set up several winners for
declarer if you play high. Even if you will never make your ace when you

---

duck, this may prove to be a good investment. Once again you are sitting East for this deal:

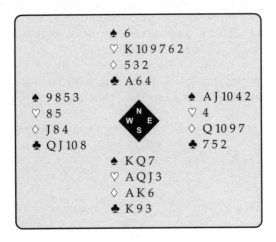

```
                    ♠ 6
                    ♡ K 10 9 7 6 2
                    ◇ 5 3 2
                    ♣ A 6 4
    ♠ 9 8 5 3                      ♠ A J 10 4 2
    ♡ 8 5              N            ♡ 4
    ◇ J 8 4        W     E          ◇ Q 10 9 7
    ♣ Q J 10 8        S             ♣ 7 5 2
                    ♠ K Q 7
                    ♡ A Q J 3
                    ◇ A K 6
                    ♣ K 9 3
```

Against 6♡ your partner leads the ♣Q, won in the dummy. Declarer now plays the singleton ♠6. How will you defend?

You can see what will happen if you take the ace. Declarer's king and queen of spades will be set up and he will be able to throw one diamond and one club from dummy, making the slam easily.

Now let's suppose – just for the sake of argument – that you were reading a rather good book of Bridge Tips the previous evening and it recommended that you should not play your ace when a singleton was led from dummy. What would happen if you followed this learned advice and played low. The slam would go down! Declarer would not lose a spade trick, it's true, but he would have no way to avoid two minor-suit losers.

Play the pre-emptor to be short in trumps

An opponent opens with a three-bid and you nevertheless bid to a major-suit game or slam. Does the opposing opening bid affect how you should play the contract? Indeed it does. Since the pre-emptor is likely to hold seven cards in the suit that he opened, this alters the odds in each of the other suits. In particular, you should generally play the pre-emptor to be short in the trump suit. Look at this typical deal:

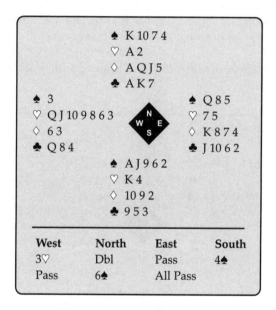

	♠ K 10 7 4	
	♡ A 2	
	◇ A Q J 5	
	♣ A K 7	

♠ 3	♠ Q 8 5
♡ Q J 10 9 8 6 3	♡ 7 5
◇ 6 3	◇ K 8 7 4
♣ Q 8 4	♣ J 10 6 2

	♠ A J 9 6 2	
	♡ K 4	
	◇ 10 9 2	
	♣ 9 5 3	

West	**North**	**East**	**South**
3♡	Dbl	Pass	4♠
Pass	6♠	All Pass	

With five cards in the other major, you are just worth a leap to 4♠ in response to partner's take-out double. Partner raises to a small slam and the ♡Q is led. How will you play the contract?

If you can pick up the trump suit without loss, success is assured. It will not matter then if the diamond finesse loses because the suit will provide a discard for your losing club. What is the most likely lie of the trump suit? If the opponents had been silent in the auction, you would usually play to drop the queen of trumps rather than finesse one or other opponent for the card. The odds in favour of playing for the drop are

---

borderline, however. If there is the slightest indication that one defender is likely to be short in the trump suit, you should finesse his partner for the queen instead. Here you have a huge indication that West is likely to be shorter than East in the trump suit. He holds seven hearts to East's two, so he is likely to be shorter than East in all three of the other suits.

After West's pre-empt, you should play a trump to dummy's king and have no hesitation in finessing East for the trump queen on the second round. Sometimes you will lose to a doubleton queen, of course, but the odds strongly favour a finesse in the long run.

There is another indication that West may hold a singleton trump on this deal. Can you think what it is? Unless West has precisely 7-2-2-2 shape, he is likely to hold a singleton somewhere in his hand. If he had a singleton in one of the minor suits, he might well have led it, seeking a ruff! The fact that he chose a heart as his opening lead strengthens even further the odds on finessing East for the trump queen.

Here is a similar deal with a different trump position. Would you have made the game?

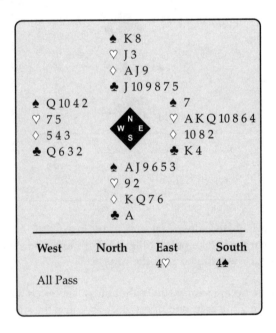

West	North	East	South
		4♡	4♠
All Pass			

West leads the ♡7 against your spade game. East cashes two rounds of the suit, West following on the second round, and switches to the ♣4. How will you play the contract?

At the table, declarer gave the play too little thought. He won the club return, played a trump to dummy's king and continued with the ♠8. East discarded a heart and the game could no longer be made. West could not be deprived of his two trump tricks.

After East's pre-empt there was every reason to fear that he might hold a singleton trump. Do you see the best play in the trump suit? On the first round you should finesse dummy's ♠8. When the cards lie as in the diagram, the finesse will win. You can then draw two further rounds with the king and ace, losing just one trump trick to the queen. It will do West no good to insert the ♠10 on the first round. You would then win with dummy's king and concede just one trump trick to West's queen.

Does the recommended play win against all possible trump singletons with East? No, it will lose to a singleton ten of trumps. However, the play will succeed against the remaining four singletons with East: queen, seven, four or two. Since it is almost impossible for East to hold four trumps (when you would do better to play the king on the first round), the odds are strongly in your favour when you finesse the ♠8. An alternative play is to run the ♠J, which would again succeed against four of the possible singletons with East, losing only to a singleton queen.

Of course, the play is right only because you can afford to lose one trump trick but not two. If the side suits were different and you needed to pick up the trump suit without loss, you would play in the normal way by cashing the king and finessing the jack.

Tip
48

Redouble to suggest playing for penalties

What should you do when your right-hand opponent makes a take-out double of your partner's one-bid and you have 10 points or more? If you choose to redouble, this should suggest playing for penalties.

Your reaction to this may be: 'Of course! What else could a redouble mean?' The point of the Tip is that you should redouble only when you have penalties in mind. Do not redouble merely because you hold 10 points or more and want to advise partner of this fact. Whenever you are short in one of the unbid suits and have no intention of defending a low-level contract there, you should not redouble. You will fare better with a descriptive (forcing) bid in a new suit.

Suppose you hold one of these East hands:

(1)	(2)	(3)
♠ 7 2	♠ J 8 2	♠ 8 4
♡ A Q 8 6 3	♡ 7 2	♡ K 5 2
◊ 8 5 2	◊ K 8 6	◊ A J 10 4 3
♣ A 6 4	♣ A Q J 8 3	♣ Q 7 5

West	North	East	South
1◊	Dbl	?	

Suppose you redouble on (1), the next player bids 1♠ and your partner doubles for penalties. Are you going to accept this as a final contract? Of course not! Why would you want to make spades trumps when you and your partner almost certainly hold at most a 4-2 fit? Since you have no intention of defending a spade contract, and that is almost certainly where the opponents are heading, you should not redouble in the first place. Bid 1♡, which should be played as forcing, and develop the auction in exactly the same way that you would have done if there had been no take-out double. This style of bidding is known as 'ignoring the double'.

On (2) you have no intention of defending against 1♡ or 1♠. So, respond 2♣ instead of redoubling. When you 'ignore the double' this response is forcing. (Many US players prefer that a one-level response is forcing but a two-level response is non-forcing. In that case they would have to redouble on the hand.)

With hand (3) you should show your diamond fit immediately. Since a raise to 3◇ would be pre-emptive, over a double, you use the artificial response of 2NT to show at least a limit raise (10+ points).

You may be wondering: 'What can go wrong if I redouble first?' Suppose you decide to redouble on hand (1), for example, and the bidding continues:

West	North	East	South
1◇	Dbl	Rdbl	1♠
Pass	2♣	?	

Not so good, is it? The bidding is uncomfortably high and you have not yet shown your hearts. A bid of 3♡ would be forcing, too. A response of 1♡ leaves you better placed and will give partner a chance to raise you.

Perhaps you are used to redoubling on all hands of 10 points or more and use a bid in a new suit as a non-forcing rescue bid, implying that you are short in partner's suit and fear the take-out double being left in for penalties. This method has been largely discarded in favour of the 'ignore the double' scheme. The first reason is that it is very unusual for the fourth player to pass the take-out double for penalties, with his trumps lying under the opener's. The second is that the opener does not need you to rescue him. Suppose you are West here:

♠ A 9 2	West	North	East	South
♡ Q 10 4 2	1◇	Dbl	Pass	Pass
◇ A 9 5 2	?			
♣ K 2				

You know that there is a huge stack of diamonds in the South hand (probably something like ◇K-Q-J-x-x) and can therefore instigate a rescue yourself. You can either remove to 1♡ or – a more flexible move – make an SOS redouble, asking partner to choose a new suit.

Tip
49

Unblock the middle card

Wﬤhen you have three cards facing five in a suit, there are various situations where the middle card in the short holding is an inconvenience. By leading the middle card on the first round, winning in the opposite hand, you can ease the run of the suit later. It's not easy to visualize, perhaps, so let's look at an example.

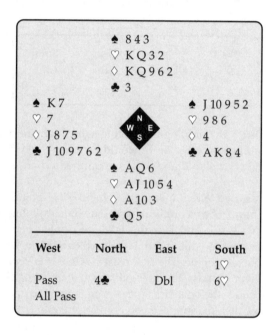

North
♠ 8 4 3
♡ K Q 3 2
◊ K Q 9 6 2
♣ 3

West
♠ K 7
♡ 7
◊ J 8 7 5
♣ J 10 9 7 6 2

East
♠ J 10 9 5 2
♡ 9 8 6
◊ 4
♣ A K 8 4

South
♠ A Q 6
♡ A J 10 5 4
◊ A 10 3
♣ Q 5

West	North	East	South
			1♡
Pass	4♣	Dbl	6♡
All Pass			

North's 4♣ is a splinter bid, showing a sound raise to game in hearts with at most one club. No-one can accuse you of underbidding when you leap immediately to a small slam. How will you play this contract when West leads the ♣J to East's ace and the ♠J is returned?

Since you are hoping to score five diamond tricks, there is no point whatsoever in risking the spade finesse. You rise with the spade ace, ruff your remaining club and draw trumps in three rounds. You must now play the diamond suit in the best way. How will you do this?

If the suit breaks 3-2, everything will be easy. If East holds ◊J-x-x-x it will be case of 'Nothing I could do, partner!' So, you must concentrate your efforts on overcoming ◊J-x-x-x with West. Suppose your first move is to lead the ◊3 to dummy's king. When you return to the ◊A, East will show out and this position will remain in the diamond suit:

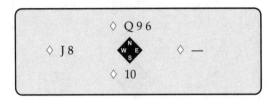

The ◊10 blocks the suit and you cannot finesse against West's ◊J. The best play in diamonds is to lead the ◊10 to dummy's king on the first round. You are unblocking the ◊10 because you can see that it might prove an encumbrance later. You return to the ◊A and the position is the suit is now a much more pleasant sight:

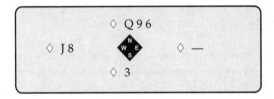

You can lead the ◊3 to dummy's ◊9 and discard your two spade losers on the queen and six of diamonds.

Sometimes an unblock will assist you only if a high card happens to fall on the first round:

You are in 3NT and long clubs lie in an otherwise entryless dummy. Your best move on the first round is to lead the ♣9 to dummy's ace. When the ♣10 (or ♣J) falls from East, a finessing position is established in the suit. You return to the ♣K and lead the ♣4 towards dummy's Q-8-6, taking the marked finesse of the 8. If you do not dispose of the ♣9 on the first round, the card will block the suit, preventing a third-round finesse.

On the next deal you must still play the middle card, even though the defenders hold a stopper in the suit.

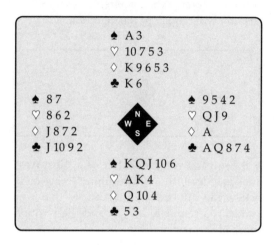

You find your way to a spade game, after East has opened 1♣, and West leads the ♣J. How will you play the contract?

There are two instructive points on this deal. The first one is that it is a clear mistake, as well as being entirely pointless, to contribute dummy's ♣K to the first trick. What will happen if you do so here? East will win with the ace, cash the ◇A and lead a low club to his partner's hand. A diamond ruff will then defeat the contract. Play low from dummy instead and you kill the entry to the West hand.

Suppose that West continues with a second round of clubs. East wins dummy's king with the ace and switches to the ♡Q. You win with the ace and must now somehow set up dummy's diamond suit for just one loser. You will then be able to discard your losing heart. How can this be done?

Since you cannot draw trumps ending in the dummy, you will need to find East with a singleton or doubleton ◇A. (If East's ace were twice guarded you would have no entry to dummy to take a discard on the fourth round of diamonds.) You draw two rounds of trumps with the king and ace and lead a low diamond from dummy. When the ace appears from East, this is no time to breathe a sigh of relief and follow with the ◇4. If you do this, you will block the diamond suit and go down. Instead you must unblock the ◇10. You can then ruff the club return and draw East's two remaining trumps. When you cash the ◇Q, seeing East show out, the way will be clear to finesse dummy's ◇9. The diamond suit is yours and you can discard your heart loser on the fourth round.

Tip 50

Do not cover an honour with an honour!

W hen you first started to play bridge, it is very likely that some kindly soul told you of a 'golden rule' of defending: always cover an honour with an honour. If you have been following this valued advice ever since, you may be surprised by the fiftieth Tip in this book: **Do not cover an honour with an honour.**

Let's look at a typical situation where covering is supposed to gain:

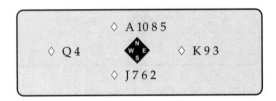

Suppose declarer leads the ◇J from his hand. If you cover with the ◇Q, sitting West, declarer will win with dummy's ace. Your partner's remaining ◇K-9 will then be worth two tricks. If instead you don't cover, East will win the ◇J with the ◇K and that is the only trick the defence will take.

Can you see what was wrong with the example we have just seen? If declarer held those cards he would not lead the jack! He would lead low to the 10, restricting his losses in the suit to one trick when you held either both the missing honours or a doubleton honour. It is fact of bridge life that when a declarer leads an honour he will nearly always welcome a cover. When a jack appears from the closed hand and you are holding the queen in second seat, the position is likely to be this:

If you cover the jack with the queen, declarer will smile inwardly and score all four tricks from the suit. If you follow the current Tip and do not cover, declarer will almost certainly conclude that your partner has the queen. He will rise with dummy's ace on this trick and run the ◇10 through East. Declarer will not 'smile inwardly' when you win with the queen. He will perhaps nod respectfully in your direction, acknowledging that you are no pushover in these two-way finesse positions. That is one good reason not to cover an honour with an honour, then. If you do cover, you may save declarer a guess.

Sometimes declarer has a guess in the trump suit. If you always 'cover an honour' you will spare him this guess. Suppose you are East here and declarer is in some high spade contract with this trump suit:

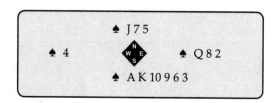

With nine trumps between the hands, declarer has no intention of taking a trump finesse. However, a skilled declarer always seeks to bend the odds in his direction. He will lead the ♠J from dummy, just in case you make the mistake of covering. You must play low, retaining your queen! What is more, you must do so without even thinking about it (or declarer may realise that you have the queen). When you do play low without a flicker, declarer will surely rise with the ace and then cash the king. Once more you will have his respect when it turns out that you started with Q-x-x and – correctly – did not cover.

It is quite possible that you will gain in this situation, too:

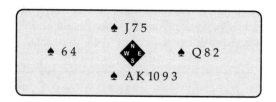

Now declarer has only eight trumps between the hands and will normally follow the 'Eight Ever, Nine Never' guideline, which tells him to finesse against the queen in this position. However, suppose he leads the ♠J from dummy and you smoothly play a low card. Declarer may think 'If East held the queen, he would have covered.' He may then rise with the ace and play the king. Having placed the queen with West, he would conclude that his only chance was to play for the queen to fall in two rounds.

Here is one more situation where a cover in the trump suit may prove disastrous:

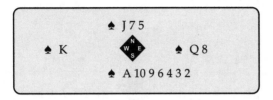

Hoping that East is an 'always cover' merchant, declarer leads the ♠J from dummy. You cover with the ♠Q and – oh dear – declarer brings in the suit without loss. This is a second way in which a cover may cost: you crash an honour in your partner's hand.

Another possibility is that by covering you will set up a second-round finesse for declarer in the suit. Take the West cards here:

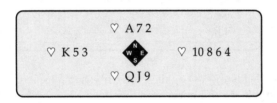

The ♡Q appears from declarer's hand. Remembering the instruction from your bridge cradle, you assume a virtuous expression and cover with the king. Do you? Look what will happen if you do cover. Declarer will win with dummy's ace and finesse the 9 on the next round. He will score three tricks in the suit!

Now suppose you recall a clever Tip that you read somewhere and refuse to cover the ♡Q. Declarer runs the queen, yes, and it wins the trick. But he can make only two tricks from the suit. If he leads the jack on the second round, you will cover with the king, promoting your partner's 10. This is in accordance with the much more sensible rule: **cover the last of touching honours.** Here you cannot actually see how many honours declarer holds. However, it is a near certainty that the queen is accompanied in declarer's hand by the jack. If he holds Q-J-10 there is nothing you can do, of course. So, assume he has two touching honours and cover on the second round, not the first.

We will end this Tip with another deal where a cover will save declarer a guess, handing him the contract on a plate. Suppose you are East here:

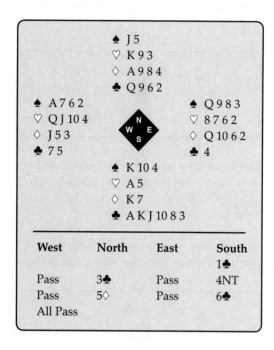

West	North	East	South
			1♣
Pass	3♣	Pass	4NT
Pass	5◇	Pass	6♣
All Pass			

Your partner leads the ♡Q against the club slam. Declarer wins, draws trumps with the ace and queen and then leads the ♠J from dummy. Are you awake in the East seat? How will you defend?

The slam depends on declarer guessing the spades correctly. When you hold the ♠Q, the winning play is to run the jack. When instead you hold the ♠A, he must rise with the king. Suppose you succumb to temptation and cover with the ♠Q... you will spare him the guess! The jack will be covered by the queen, king and ace, after which declarer can claim the contract.

It is better to follow the valuable guideline: **do not cover an honour with an honour.** When the ♠J is not covered, declarer is likely to place the ♠Q with West. In that case he will rise with the ♠K from his hand, hoping that you hold the ♠A. What bad luck!

Tip
51

**Ruff high
whenever
practical**

When you hold plenty of top trumps, you can afford to take all your ruffs in dummy with a master trump, or perhaps even draw trumps before taking your ruffs. When your trumps are not so strong, you may have a decision to take — should I ruff high, to avoid an overruff, or should I ruff low and keep the trump honour to protect myself against a bad trump break? Look at this deal:

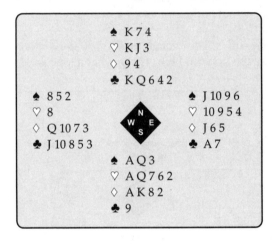

West leads the ♣J against your contract of 6♡. You cover with the ♣K and East takes the ace, returning the ♠J. How will you play the contract?

One of the diamond losers can be thrown on the ♣Q. What plans can you make for the other one? Setting up a long club is not particularly promising. Even if the clubs break 4-3, you will need to take two club ruffs in the long trump holding and this will lead to defeat whenever the trumps break 4-1. A better idea is to ruff one of your diamond losers in dummy. How does the play go?

You win the spade switch with the ace, cash the ace and king of diamonds and lead a third round of the suit, West following with the 10. Should you ruff with a high trump (the king or jack) or with a low trump? If you ruff high, you will avoid the risk of an overruff by East. However, you will then lose a trump trick whenever the trumps break 4-1.

The risk of a 5-2 break (in diamonds) is roughly similar to that for a 4-1 break (in trumps), at around 30%. Nevertheless, it is much better to ruff low and risk an overruff. Do you see why? Firstly, half of the 30% for a 5-2 diamond break arises when West has the doubleton. So, the chance of East having a doubleton diamond is only 15%. Secondly, if West held ◊Q-J-10-x-x, he might have led the suit. So you ruff low, East following, and cash the king and jack of trumps. You then return to hand with the ♠Q and draw East's remaining trumps. Finally you can return to dummy with the ♠K to discard your last diamond on the ♣Q.

Suppose you have two ruffs to take in dummy and cannot afford an overruff. If dummy holds only one top trump, you will obviously take the first ruff with a low trump (when the risk of an overruff is less). You save the top trump for the second ruff, when it is more likely one of the defenders will be out of the suit you are ruffing.

When only one ruff will be enough to give you the contract, the safe line may be to take the first ruff high. That's what happens here:

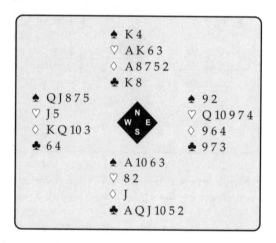

```
                    ♠ K 4
                    ♡ A K 6 3
                    ◊ A 8 7 5 2
                    ♣ K 8
  ♠ Q J 8 7 5                      ♠ 9 2
  ♡ J 5              N             ♡ Q 10 9 7 4
  ◊ K Q 10 3      W     E          ◊ 9 6 4
  ♣ 6 4              S             ♣ 9 7 3
                    ♠ A 10 6 3
                    ♡ 8 2
                    ◊ J
                    ♣ A Q J 10 5 2
```

West leads the ◊K against 6♣. How will you play the contract?

You have eleven tricks on top. If you were in 7♣, you would need to ruff both losing spades. You would ruff the third round with the ♣8 and the fourth round with the ♣K. You would ruff with the low trump when there was less risk of an overruff.

Playing in 6♣, you need only one spade ruff. Look what will happen if you ruff the third round of spades with the ♣8. East will overruff with the ♣9 and return a trump. You will go down! To play safe in the small slam, you must take the first ruff with ♣K. You can then draw trumps and concede a spade trick at the end. Small slam made! (Or you can seek an overtrick by ruffing the fourth spade with the ♣8, which will not succeed as the cards lie.)

Sometimes it can be beneficial to ruff with a trump that is high but not a master. You gain when a defender has no more cards in the side suit but cannot overruff because he does not hold a higher trump. Look at this deal:

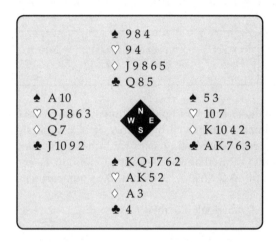

West leads the ♣J against 4♠. How would you plan the play?

A trump switch will not aid your prospects, so you play low in dummy, leaving West on lead. As you had hoped, he misses the trump switch and continues with another club. What now?

You ruff in the South hand and must now ruff your two heart losers. You cash the ace and king of the suit and ruff the third round of hearts with the ♠9. East has no hearts left but cannot overruff with the ♠10. (You wouldn't mind if he overruffed with the ace. If he then returned a trump, you would win and ruff your last heart with the ♠8.) You return to your hand with the ◊A and ruff your last heart with the ♠8. Finally you lead a trump, eventually emerging with ten tricks.

Tip 52

When a pre-empt is doubled suggest an opening lead

Your partner opens with a pre-empt, either a weak two or a weak three, and the next player doubles for take-out. What should it mean if you bid a new suit now, in an auction such as this:

West	North	East	South
3♡	Dbl	4♣	

It is very unlikely that you hold a club suit that rivals the seven-card heart suit already announced by opener. It is also barely possible that your hand merits some sort of slam try in hearts. In the above auction your 4♣ should mean that you are happy to raise to 4♡ and that, if South should attempt 4♠ (or 5◇), you would like your partner to lead a club.

The whole deal may look like this:

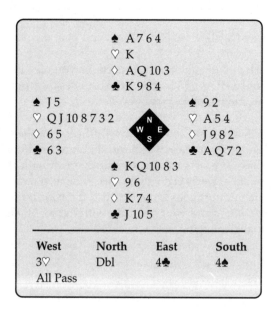

```
                        ♠ A 7 6 4
                        ♡ K
                        ◇ A Q 10 3
                        ♣ K 9 8 4
    ♠ J 5                              ♠ 9 2
    ♡ Q J 10 8 7 3 2       N          ♡ A 5 4
    ◇ 6 5              W       E       ◇ J 9 8 2
    ♣ 6 3                  S           ♣ A Q 7 2
                        ♠ K Q 10 8 3
                        ♡ 9 6
                        ◇ K 7 4
                        ♣ J 10 5
```

West	North	East	South
3♡	Dbl	4♣	4♠
All Pass			

South does bid 4♠, as you rather expected, and your partner will now

---

52 Great Bridge Tips

lead a club instead of a heart. You will take two club tricks, cash the ♡A and deliver a club ruff. One down! Without a club lead, declarer would have made the contract easily.

Here is an example of the method after a weak-two opening:

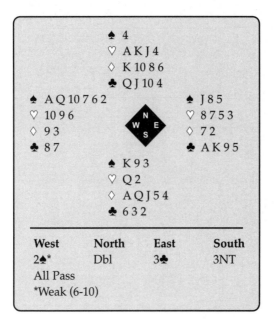

	♠ 4		
	♡ A K J 4		
	◇ K 10 8 6		
	♣ Q J 10 4		

	♠ 4		
♠ A Q 10 7 6 2		♠ J 8 5
♡ 10 9 6	N	♡ 8 7 5 3
◇ 9 3	W E	◇ 7 2
♣ 8 7	S	♣ A K 9 5

	♠ K 9 3		
	♡ Q 2		
	◇ A Q J 5 4		
	♣ 6 3 2		

West	North	East	South
2♠*	Dbl	3♣	3NT
All Pass			
*Weak (6-10)			

If South decides to attempt 3NT, despite the lead-directing 3♣ bid, he will suffer a heavy defeat. After a club lead to East's king, followed by a switch to the ♠J the defenders will score the first eight tricks for four down. Suppose East is not playing the method and raises to 3♠ instead. It will not then be at all easy for West to find the killing club lead.

Don't you hate it when bridge writers show you deals that fit their suggested methods so perfectly? On the above two deals the benefit of the lead-directing bid was enormous. West was told of the killing lead and the contract tumbled to defeat. Just as often, the effect of the lead-directing bid will be less spectacular, perhaps preventing an overtrick in a Pairs event. We bridge players need all the assistance we can get, though, and I hope that this Tip, along with all the others in the book, will work well for you.

Good luck next time you take your seat at a bridge table – the world's greatest sporting arena!